BREEDING PUREBRED CATS

Breeding Purebred Cats

*A Guide for the Novice
and Small Breeder*

by Anne S. Moore

ABRAXAS PUBLISHING · BELLEVUE, WASHINGTON

Library of Congress Cataloging in Publication Data

Moore, Anne S., 1949 -
Breeding purebred cats.

Includes index.
1. Cats – Breeding.   I. Title.
SF447.5.M66   636.8'082   81-66811
ISBN 0-939768-00-3   AACR2

ISBN 0-939768-00-3

Library of Congress Catalog Number 81-66811

©1981 by Susan D Tartaglino
First published 1981
Second impression 1982
Third impression 1983
Revised edition ©1988

Cover illustration:
Theophile-Alexandre Steinlen (1859-1923)

Printed in the United States of America

Abraxas Publishing
P.O. Box 1522
Bellevue, Washington 98009
10245 Main Street
Bellevue, Washington 98004

Table of Contents

Introduction

There are people who breed cats and people who let cats breed.

It's a simple matter to throw two cats together and hope for the best. But somewhere down the road, disaster and disappointment await the person who believes that "nature" will take care of everything.

The mark of the serious breeder is her devotion to the welfare of every cat and kitten that passes through her hands, whether those number one hundred or only one. Such a breeder demands of herself an ever-growing knowledge of a species hardly lass complex than our own.

Yet all too often, the person starting out in cats has no one to help her through the first few years. She might spend months in locating an experienced breeder. Once found, that person may attempt to discourage the newcomer, whether from fear of declining market values, dislike of competition, or just the feeling that no novice can breed cats with integrity and intelligence. The experienced breeder who *is* willing to help will not have time to answer all the questions that arise, even if the novice knows what questions need to be asked. There are, of course, hundreds of books about cats, but these are oriented toward the pet owner, not the breeder.

Breeding Purebred Cats was written for the novice and small breeder. It covers the mechanics of breeding, breeding systems, and cattery management. It offers suggestions on the purchase of foundation stock, showing, standard sale and stud arrangements, and many other practical matters. Aspects of the cat that have been covered *ad infinitum* in a myriad of other cat books have been avoided – such as general cat care and descriptions of all the breeds. My favorites of these many books are listed in the back.

Women dominate cat breeding, as they dominate almost all types of exhibition-animal breeding. Therefore I refer to cat breeders in the feminine. Lest the men feel left out, cat judges and veterinarians are referred to in the masculine.

*"Dieu a fait le chat pour donner à
l'homme le plaisir de caresser le tigre."*

(God made the cat to give man the joy of
caressing the tiger.)

—*Méry*

Cats as pets

An estimated one household in four owns a cat; one in one hundred owns a purebred cat. Many households, of course, own a representative of "man's best friend." But cats have been catching up, and recently the pet industry has announced that the cat has passed the dog as America's most popular pet.

It's easy to see why. In a society more and more oriented towards convenience products, cats fill the need for a convenience pet. They are relatively undemanding, they keep themselves tidy and clean, they are inoffensive to the neighbors and, being small, relatively cheap to feed. They are tremendously adaptable and, because they make excellent use of space, are perfect townhouse or apartment pets. At the same time, they offer as much individuality, affection and companionship as dogs, however different their basic personality may be.

Cats also have a certain cachet. Traditionally they are the companions of writers and intellectuals. They are creatures of beauty and mystery that are still true to their wild natures: the tigers in the house.

Recent studies have shown that the keeping of cats and other animals as pets can help alleviate mental stress and promote longevity in their owners.

All these reasons point toward the continuing popularity of cats as pets. But what about the *purebred* cat? After all, puppy buyers almost always think in terms of a particular breed; kitten buyers do not. The reasons for purchasing a particular breed, however, apply to both. Except for the hunting breeds, few people buy a dog breed for its original purpose. The city dweller has no flocks of sheep to tend and probably has never heard of bull-baiting, but the Sheltie and the Bulldog are still around. Their owners value them for their appearance and their personalities. In the same way, the cat breeds will be valued not only by the status-seeker, but by those who appreciate their special look and temperament.

The population problem

Some people find cats attractive as pets because they imagine that cats can fend for themselves. They feel no guilt over abandoning a cat, whereas they would never think of leaving their faithful, vulnerable dog to its own devices. Such people will seek out strays and free kittens; they will not answer ads for purebreds – a reason good enough in itself for breeding only purebreds.

Unfortunately, cats *are* expendable in our society. Hundreds are killed daily at public expense, while their former owners (if any) wonder about the kitten that "ran away." Some cat owners take their pets to animal shelters, easing their feelings of guilt with the thought that someone will adopt them.

No cat breeder likes to be reminded of the overpopulation problem that she is adding to, yet it is a situation we must all face. "If only all breeding were licensed and controlled," some will say. Though tentative moves in this direction have been made by some communities, the impossibility of enforcement is enough to insure that restrictive laws will not be passed on any widespread basis.

What, then, can the breeder do? She should first insist on an alteration agreement for every pet kitten she sells, and she should *follow up* to be sure it's been adhered to. She should sell cats for breeding only after scrutiny of the buyer's aims and ideas. She should investigate every home into which her kittens are sold, and ask to be notified if the buyer ever sells or gives away the cat. She can even offer to help find a home: stressing this point will keep the kittens you've produced from ever facing abandonment. Within the first few months of selling a kitten, she should keep in touch with the buyer and offer advice on any problems. Anything she can do to instruct her kitten customers will help her own kittens as well as cats in general.

The breeder must be certain that every kitten she sells passes into loving, responsible ownership — and if such homes cease to be available, she must stop breeding cats.

But she should never feel guilty about her hobby. If all kittens were the products of controlled breedings, carefully raised and carefully sold by breeders such as the one described, the cat population crisis would be at an end.

Exhibition breeding

Animals have been bred selectively for thousands of years, but the history of exhibition breeding is limited to the last century.

A breed is a group of animals distinguished from others of their species by characteristics which they will pass on to their progeny when interbred. Breeds have been created by man for three reasons: performance, production and aesthetics.

From their wild progenitors man has selected horses according to their pulling capacity, their weight-carrying ability, or their speed. Most dog breeds, too, were originally bred for specific performance functions, as their names often illustrate: Scottish Deerhound, Russian Wolfhound.

Production breeds have been selected for increased yield in milk or eggs or meat: our food animals.

But exhibition breeding is something quite new. In the nineteeth century, the Victorians discovered a mania for exhibitions and, at the same time, an empathy with animals as sentient beings. One result was the emergence of humane societies, another was the birth of animal exhibitions. The first exhibition cats were not purebreds – purebred cats did not exist, in our modern sense of the word – and a cat of unusual size or markings or coloration could be a top show winner.

The breeding of animals for exhibition has swept across every species of domestic animal and resulted in an abundance of new breeds. Rabbits, chickens, ducks, guppies, mice, cavies, pigeons, dogs, cats; just about anything that can be bred and shown *is* bred and shown.

Cats as a medium for the breeder's art

Unlike other domestic animals, the cat has never been bred for performance or production. The cat's only performance expertise has been in rodent control, and man has always shown more interest in building a better mousetrap than in breeding a better mouser. And the cat's only product is — more cats.

Because cat breeding is so new, the species offers tremedous challenges and opportunities. Horses and dogs come in all sizes and shapes. Cats do not — not yet — but they will. The species comprises a stunning variety of colors, patterns, coat textures and conformation types. Already the popular colorpoint pattern has been bred into traditional breeds to create the Himalayan, Si-Manx and Si-Rex, while the Siamese breeders have picked up other colors to give us colorpoint shorthairs in red, cream, tortoiseshell, blue-cream and all the colors of tabby. Long hair has been added to the slim, svelte body type of the Siamese and short hair bred onto the cobby body of the Persian. Other breeders are incorporating the wild-cat coat patterns into the domestic cat; still others are breeding cats with folded ears, curled ears, bobbed tails or wiry coats. Whatever new combination can be imagined, someone is probably working on it.

Looking ahead thirty years or so, one can visualize miniature cats, spotted cats, striped cats, cats in all colors, textures, patterns, shapes and sizes.

The appearance of the breeds

Some breed enthusiasts try to claim great antiquity for their chosen breed, but they're whistling in the wind. Modern cat breeding originated about a hundred years ago as a result of exhibitions. Some breeds have been "naturally" created by geographic restriction combined with local mutation, as in the Manx or Siamese. Such cats may have been popular and valuable animals, but no records exist to prove that they were ever selectively bred towards a true breed standard.

In a free-breeding population of cats, two distinct types are visible: the first has a streamlined body and wedge-shaped head, as in today's Siamese, the second has a cobby body and broad, domed skull, like the Persian. These two types are carried to the extremes seen at today's shows only by selective breeding.

Breed standards

Man's idea of aesthetic perfection in the "using" animals grew out of his performance requirements. In the horse, for example, straight pasterns and a long back are considered faults not because they are unsightly but because the first is accompanied by stiff gaits and the second by weakness under weight.

In standards created for aesthetic reasons there can be no such criteria, and requirements of conformation and color become wholly arbitrary. There is, therefore, nothing sacrosanct about breed standards. They're created by individuals around a mutually agreed upon image of the ideal.

If the standards are slow to change, it's for good reason. Animal breeding is a slow process. Change the goals too soon and breeders will throw up their hands in despair. On the other hand, breed standards should not be regarded as immutable; in fact, they *must* change as the goals and visions of breeders evolve. There is no Perfect Cat towards which all breeders slowly progress, for hardly have we defined that perfection than we look beyond it. Likewise, breeders who prefer the old-fashioned type of their breed should not be despised, for today's type is "better" only because a majority of breeders and judges have agreed to make it so. Who knows? In another fifty years we might come full circle, and that old-fashioned type might become the new look.

However, a breeder should depart from current standards only after thorough study of the breed and the most careful consideration. The novice breeder should decide at the outset to breed only those cats that are currently competitive in the show ring, for reasons I'll explain later.

If you see a cat of your chosen breed that you consider quite ugly, and yet it is winning at all the shows, don't be discouraged. Bear in mind that a great variety of looks is possible within any breed. Study the photos of twenty grand champions of any breed and you'll discover some surprising differences. The breed standards are general enough that they can admit a wide range of interpretation by both breeder and judge. Gradually, a certain look or type will come more into favor, and this will in turn lead to new variations.

The most successful breeders are those who are always looking ahead, who are able to predict what the future will demand in their particular breed. Or, they are breeders who breed for a look that *they* like, and, once they've produced it, happily discover that the judges like it too.

The pedigree: names and titles

A pedigree is a piece of paper filled with the names of cats – that is, we must assume them to be cats, for unless we know the individuals listed they may be jackrabbits or cocker spaniels. A pedigree tells us little about the merits of the individual, but provides valuable clues to its breeding potential. The titles of the cats on a pedigree mean as little as the names unless we know more about them. What association were the wins in, what area, what year? Did the cat become a champion in competition or by default?

My point here: don't be impressed by a long line of fancy names on a pedigree. Any alleycat can have a pedigree, if only someone will bother to write it down.

The pedigrees of a novice breeder's first cats will probably mean little to her, yet their importance increases the further she progresses in the fancy. Therefore, she should make every effort to get a complete, five-generation pedigree including colors and registration numbers with every kitten or cat she buys.

The names appearing on a pedigree are the registered names of a cat's ancestors. The first part of each name will be the registered cattery name of the person who bred the cat — the owner of the queen at the time of mating. (In dogs, the breeder's kennel name can appear as a prefix or a suffix; i.e., Sunshine's Fido, or Fido of Sunshine, but in cats it must appear as a prefix.) All this person's kittens will be registered under the same name. Every serious breeder will have a cattery name, though it may not be registered with all the different associations. It costs around $35 to register the name with each association.

The novice breeder should decide upon a cattery name right away and register it with CFA, even though her first litter of kittens is far in the future. CFA is the largest association and has the most cattery names registered, so recording your cattery name there first will help prevent the misfortune of having different cattery names in various associations. After the name is accepted by CFA, have it registered with the other associations in which you're likely to be showing your cats. Be prepared for your third or fourth choice to be the one assigned, for the name you want may well have been chosen already by someone else. One popular idea is to make a cattery name out of one's own name or an anagram of it. You need not even own a cat to register a cattery name. Simply write to the association for the correct form. Once you have registered your cattery name, all your kittens registered with that association will carry your cattery prefix. Kittens can still be registered in other associations — those in which your cattery name is *not* registered — but your cattery name cannot be included. This is why the same cat may be registered in several associations and have a different name in each one.

You may see cats listed in a pedigree, or even at the shows, that have no cattery name. This is unfortunate and unprofessional on the part of the breeder. Once you become familiar with the various bloodlines in your breed, a cattery name will have meaning where the name of the individual cat will not. For example, if a cattery name appears that belongs to someone known to use only top-class breeding stock, we can assume that the cats under that name are excellent producers, even though we have never seen them and they were never shown. Other cattery names can be found "hidden" in a pedigree if we know the bloodlines of our breed. We may see four or five different cattery names on a pedigree, for instance, and know that they all trace back to a particularly distinguished line that is farther back than the pedigree can show. A three-generation pedigree can represent as little as four years of breeding. Our interest in the cat's ancestors should go back farther than this.

The second part of a cat's registered name is its individual name. This name must be different from all other individual names registered under that cattery prefix. Some breeders with a limited selection of names get around this by adding numerals, e.g., Max I, Max II, and Max III. There are few restrictions except in length: the sum of all letters in a cat's registered name must fall within about twenty-six letters, depending on the association.

Space permitting, the purchaser of a purebred kitten can add his cattery name after the breeder's cattery name and the individual name. Again, this can be done only if the cattery name to be suffixed is registered with the association to which you are applying, and if it falls within the letter allowance. The letter allowance is one reason to keep your cattery name as short as possible. If you purchase a cat that already has a cattery suffix (that is, from a cattery other than the original breeder's), you can sometimes change the cattery suffix to your own cattery name, depending on the association. Regulations for transfer of ownership will include this information.

It is not *necessary* to add your cattery name to the name of a cat you've purchased, but most people do, especially if they plan to show the cat. The cattery suffix is added to the registration certificate when the transfer of ownership is sent to the association.

For example: a cat named "Larkspur's Red Sun of Purrlific" was bred by the owner of the Larkspur Cattery and was purchased by the owner of the Purrlific Cattery, although he may now be owned by a different cattery. Since the name of a color (red) is part of the cat's name, the cat must be a red.

Titles on a CFA pedigree may include Champion (Ch) and Grand Champion (GC). Some associations have additional titles; for example: Double, Triple, and Quadruple Champion; Double, Triple, Quadruple and Supreme Grand Champion, and so forth. Older pedigrees may contain titles no longer in existence, such as ACFA's Royal Merit (RM), awarded on the basis of a scoring system that is no longer used. Distinguished Merit (DM) or a similar title is suffixed to the names of cats which have produced five Grand Champions (for a female) or fifteen Grand Champions (for a male). Distinguished Merit is the most prestigious title of all, for it indicates a cat that has consistently produced top-show progeny, and a bloodline of exceptional quality.

Colors and registration numbers on pedigrees

Most pedigrees will list the colors of the cat's ancestors on the pedigree after or beneath each cat's name. Once you are familiar with the color genetics of your breed, this information will tell you whether the kitten you purchased carries any colors as recessives, either as a certainty or as a probability. If your black female kitten is the product of a black x blue (recessive) breeding, then the kitten *must* carry a gene for blue, and can produce blue kittens as well as the dominant black, depending also, of course, on the color of the stud cat used. Recessives can be carried unseen through many, many generations. If your kitten is the product of black x black matings except for one blue great-grand-mother, there is still a chance (about 12%) that she will carry blue. Cat breeding is based on probabilities, and it is possible, based on a pedigree, to work out the probabilities for a cat's carrying various colors or patterns that are recessive, as well as other traits such as coat length — longhair being recessive to short.

Until you have a thorough understanding of your breed's genetics, you should review a new kitten's pedigree with the breeder to determine what colors you can expect when breeding her, if this is important to you. Novice breeders often want to produce as many different colors as possible. Many breeders, especially in the most popular breeds, wisely decide to specialize in one particular color or color group.

Registration numbers are usually written onto pedigrees. Although you may not think it important at first (after all, your kitten's number and the numbers of her parents are on your registration certificate), you should make an effort to get these numbers. They are available from the registering association for a fee of $25 to $35. Why might you need them in the future?

Perhaps your kitten is registered in CFA. You decide to show primarily in another association, however, and must now register her in that association. You may be required to furnish a three-generation pedigree with all registration numbers in order to register your kitten in the new association. A copy of the registration certificate is not enough. If you don't already have the numbers, you will have to pay for a certified pedigree.

How are kittens registered? The breeder of a litter will register the entire litter with CFA, and will receive a "blue slip" for each kitten. (She may or may not register with another association at the same time.) The blue slip will be returned to the association by the new owner for individual registration of the cat.

Pedigree falsification

Novices tend to disregard the pedigrees of their first cats. After all, beyond a few titles and colors, the pedigrees are more or less meaningless. But the longer you stay in the cat fancy, the more valuable the pedigree will become. At a recent show, I watched another exhibitor who was kitten shopping spend two minutes examining a kitten and twenty minutes examining its pedigree. And many very experienced breeders work almost entirely from pedigrees; that is, they will select cats for breeding on the basis of their pedigrees alone.

Therefore, the accuracy of pedigrees is of the utmost importance. All breeders are dismayed and alarmed to hear rumors of pedigree falsification, which invalidates a pedigree not just for the cat involved, but for all future generations bred from that cat.

What about the certified pedigree available from the associations? Unfortunately, its legitimacy is only semantic. A certified pedigree is no more valid than one written by a breeder, since the breeders are the only source of information for the registering associations.

Why might a breeder falsify a pedigree? There are several situations that may tempt her to do so. Perhaps she has a famous stud cat that has lost interest in breeding, but his offspring are much more valuable than those of her other males. Perhaps she has tried a shortcut to breed improvement by the "illegal" use of another breed. Perhaps she has a kitten that is the result of a perfectly legitimate breeding program, and can itself be used for breeding, but cannot be shown (such as a longhair Exotic Shorthair); she would like to be able to show it, but can do so only if she "adjusts" the pedigree.

Probably more common is accidental falsification. Breeders with more than one stud may forget to which one a queen was bred, or may not even know. They may have a queen in with one stud for days and discover, when the kittens are at last produced, that another stud who only had access to her for thirty seconds is the father of her litter. And, of course, a litter may easily have more than one sire. It's a little harder to forget who the mother of each kitten is, but this has happened too. Sometimes mistakes do not become evident until the second generation, when an "impossible" color or pattern is produced.

Despite the rumors – and proof – of pedigree falsification, the great majority of breeders are both ethical and accurate in making out pedigrees. The novice breeder, especially if she has more than one male, must be extremely careful in her record keeping and the handling of her cats, so that her own pedigrees never fall under suspicion.

The flash-in-the-pan breeder

The life-cycle of the average cat breeder follows a predictable pattern. The breeder buys her first purebred kitten. She might not be thinking of breeding when she buys the kitten, or she might want to breed just one litter. Sometimes she's discouraged from breeding by the kitten's breeder or her friends, or she might be unable to find a stud of the same breed, or the cost might be too high.

But perhaps she goes ahead and raises a litter or two. Now she discovers that her breed is popular and she has no trouble selling the kittens — in fact, she makes a tidy sum. Looking for somewhere to spend the money, she thinks, why not another breeding female, or possibly a male? She goes to some cat shows and buys a good-quality kitten. A few months later, having experienced the heady feeling of winning a few ribbons, her motivation has shifted from raising kittens for fun and a little profit to winning ribbons. Now she wants to produce her *own* show winners. The cat population quickly expands.

The next year, she has some good kittens of her own breeding to show, and perhaps they do well. She keeps or buys still more kittens and soon has a breeding population of twenty to forty cats.

Then, perhaps, the quality of her kittens falls off or her cattery is struck by disease or her breeding stock suddenly fails to produce. It isn't as easy as she thought it was going to be to produce top kittens. She hadn't anticipated such problems and now she has to meet them, not with two or three cats, but with twenty or thirty. She sells off her breeding stock and spays a couple of favorites to keep as pets.

This scenario is not meant to discourage, but to inform. (For one thing, it may help you understand why serious breeders are reluctant to sell a top kitten to a novice breeder.)There are many breeders who have spent their lives in the cat fancy. If you don't learn from the mistakes of others you will repeat them yourself.

The prices of purebred cats

Compared to dogs, cats are much cheaper to keep in terms of food and space requirements, while the price of purebred kittens approaches that of purebred pups. Some breeds will cost more if they are in great demand, or if breeders have banded together to "fix" prices.

The current prices for registered purebred kittens currently fall into the following ranges: pets, $175 to $300, breeding quality, $250 to $650, and show quality, $500 to $1000 and up — *way* up. The large range and overlap reflect the differing popularity of certain breeds and the higher prices charged in some parts of the country. In one particular area, for one particular breed, the range will be much narrower. Every breeder should keep in touch with others in her area to be sure that her prices stay in line.

The price range for show quality kittens is always large, for a show quality kitten can be anything from the one that "might do something at the shows" to the one that'll set the show world on fire. Those members of the public who quail at the thought of paying $200 for a pet kitten and go into shock at the idea of forking over $350 for a breeding cat would probably collapse in a coma if they knew the prices paid for the superstars. The prices of superstar adults that are proven producers will be even higher, soaring well into five figures.

Terminology

Mature cats are either *altered* or *entire*. A male alter is a *neuter*, a female alter is a *spay*. An entire male is a *tom* or *stud*; an entire female is a *queen*. Some breeders refer to their cats as "boys" and "girls." A *maiden* female is one that has never produced a litter. An *open* female is one that has not been bred since her last litter or is not pregnant.

A young cat is a male or female *kitten* until maturity, which is arbitrarily fixed at eight months. Parturition in the cat is *kittening* (occasionally one sees the incorrect *whelping*). Copulation is *mating* or *breeding*; the male's activity is *siring*, though, if he could talk, the tom might not agree that he's doing it just to sire kittens.

A cat that is not a *purebred* is called at the shows a *household pet (HHP)*. *Mixed-breed* and *mongrel* are sometimes heard, but properly apply to dogs. The non-purebred is also called a *domestic*.

In referring to a kitten's parentage, it is correctly said to be *out of* the female and *by* the male.

Terms associated with genetics will be defined later.

Qualifications for breeding cats

Breeding purebred cats is a hobby open to almost everyone, but there are a few qualifying factors. Your financial resources should extend well beyond the purchase of foundation stock and stud fees, for you must also consider the cost of pre-mating checkups, vaccinations of both queen and kittens, advertising, and showing. You must also be prepared for the inevitable health problems and high veterinary costs that *will* arise somewhere along the way, if not tomorrow.

Emergency care *must* be available if your queen should require a caesarean or if a young kitten swallows poison. The home environment should be quiet and secure, with enough space for the number of cats you intend to keep.

It is not necessary that you be available twenty-four hours a day — many breeders hold full-time jobs — but it *is* important that you be able to take time off from work if necessary, and if you can drive home during your lunch hour to check on a queen about to give birth, so much the better.

If you are in a remote country area, it will be more difficult to sell your kittens.

Do you move a lot? If so, you will have to limit your animals to a very few, and you must also consider that cats will require time to adjust to each new home and might refuse to breed at first. Cats become very dependent on their home environments.

Finally, you must have the time and willingness to sit up all night as a cat midwife, to nurse frail kittens back to health, to care for orphans, and to locate good homes for your kittens.

Attitudes

The attitude of cat lovers towards their pets changes hardly at all when they make the transition to cat breeders. Few consider that with several animals they will not be able to continue an intimate relationship with each individual, nor will they be able to keep every cat throughout its lifespan. Non-productive cats can remain as pets only at the expense of the breeding program, unless space is unlimited — and with cats, the rule seems to be: cats expand to fill the space available, and then some! Nor can the breeder afford to be hypochondriac concerning her stock, or her vet bill will reach staggering proportions. And no longer can she cater to the likes and dislikes of each cat.

In commercial and large-scale catteries, the cats are caged and generally well cared for because of their value as breeding stock. They become cat-oriented rather than people-oriented because they get little affection from humans. They are sold or given away when their productive life is over or if they fail to produce quality kittens.

The majority of cat breeders feel, conversely, that each and every cat needs strong human ties and must never be sold or given away, caged, or put to sleep, even if she becomes senile and pees on the pillow every night.

Don't jump to the conclusion that one point of view is better than the other. What *is* cruel is to accustom a young cat to lots of daily attention and then suddenly withdraw it when he matures by putting him out with a lot of strange cats. If a cat is destined to be one of many, don't let him feel that he has exclusive rights to your attention, and be sure he doesn't grow up alone or he may never learn to interact socially with other cats.

Many cats in large-scale breeding operations lead lives of luxury. They are often better cared for than most pets, and the large-scale breeder should certainly not be disparaged. But if you believe that cats should be beloved pets first and breeding animals second, you should carefully consider your attitudes before you begin. Otherwise you may find yourself one day with an unwieldy, time-consuming business you never wanted, and cats you haven't bothered to name.

The function of the cat breeder

Ask a serious breeder why she is breeding cats (outside of personal satisfaction) and she will almost always come up with something about improvement of the breed. This has been the banner of animal breeders for a long time, but alas, it means little when applied to cats. A performance or production animal *can* be improved; our racehorses are faster and our chickens lay more eggs than their ancestors did one hundred years ago. But how can we speak of *improving* an animal that is bred for appearance alone? Is a cat with a short nose an improvement over a cat with an extremely long nose? The Persian breeder would say that it is, the Siamese breeder would disagree, and the vet would probably not like either one of them.

The animal with the greatest potential in terms of health and adaptability is the domestic, heterozygous cat. The breeder of purebreds should drop the illusion that she's doing something beneficial for cats. We've only to look at what some of our neighbors in dog breeding are producing to know that, in many cases, "bettering the breed" merges all too easily into worsening the species.

Other breeders, particularly those interested in the unusual breeds, imagine that they're doing a good deed in preserving a rare variety of animal. They are confusing breeds with species. *Any* breed of cat can be re-created from the genetic material in the general population of cats within a few generations of breeding, though some of the fine points may take longer to regain. Even entire species of animals have been re-created or saved from extinction by making use of closely related species and hybrids: the European bison is one example.

What, then, is the function of the cat breeder? First, she is providing pet owners with healthy, well-cared-for kittens that will fulfill expectations in terms of disposition and appearance. Second, she is creating a living creature of great beauty. And third, through providing expert advice to her customers and through showing her cats, she is promoting the welfare of all cats.

On being professional

Cat hobbyists generally refuse to regard breeding as a business, though all the ingredients are there: a product, an inventory, sales to the public, exhibitions, advertising and promotion. The cat fancy has picked up some of the faults of the business world — back-stabbing, fraud, and libel — and could benefit from some of its virtues — fair, competitive pricing, guarantees that really mean something, accurate record-keeping, and clearly-defined, written agreements.

Too many breeders eschew anything that smacks of "business," and breeders are even accused of being *too* professional, whatever that may mean. Certainly every breeder should be professional in outlook, whether her cattery remains a hobby or becomes a business.

When starting out, you might want to discuss with an accountant the possibility of declaring your cattery a business. This decision should be made at the outset, since your largest expenses will be incurred then.

Chapter Two: *Breeding Stock*

Only registered purebreds should be used for breeding

The novice breeder should decide at the outset to breed only purebred, registered cats from bloodlines that are currently competitive in the show ring.

No one quite agrees on what is "better" in a breed, and a purebred is superior to a domestic cat only if it is more to our taste in appearance or temperament. Why, then, should the cat breeder not work with domestics?

It's regrettable that the purebred should be valued over the domestic, but such is the case. The purebred kitten has a far better chance of finding a loving, responsible and permanent home than the domestic. For this reason, if for no other, the breeder should not allow her domestic cats to produce kittens.

An alternative that seems to be gaining in popularity is the breeding of cats that are purebred but not registered. Such breeders heap scorn on the "piece of paper," and persuade their customers that the registration certificate has no value if they're only buying a pet.

This is a mistake that perpetuates itself. Many of the kittens that are advertised in newspapers turn out to be the progeny of unregistered breedings, and there are even some large-scale breeders who work with unregistered cats.

Early in your hobby career you may be tempted to purchase a purebred non-registered kitten to use for breeding. Perhaps it is the only kitten of your chosen breed you've been able to locate. Perhaps you're not interested in showing, and are not convinced of the value of the registration. Then too, non-registered kittens are usually sold at lower prices, and without the alteration conditions attached to pet kitten sales by serious breeders.

There may be another reason you're considering breeding non-registered purebreds. You may have purchased a pet kitten from a breeder of registered stock without the papers. But you've since become interested in breeding, so why not use the already-mature female at hand? The breeder, you may think, will be too busy to remember you and after all, you're not asking for the papers, are you?

If you find yourself in such a situation you should call the breeder and talk the problem over with her. Your kitten may come from excellent bloodlines; she may even have been a breeding-quality kitten to start with or may have developed into one. The breeder might be willing to give you the papers — she may want to see the mature cat to determine how it's developed — and you will probably have to pay an additional sum: the difference between a pet kitten and a breeding kitten. Or maybe the breeder will insist that you live up to the original agreement. If you said you would alter the kitten, you have no choice but to comply.

So, why *not* breed non-registered purebreds? Many of the people who buy your pet kittens will not care whether they are registered or not.

Consider, first, the difficulty of obtaining stud service for your non-registered queen. (It can be difficult enough to find stud service for a *registered* queen). Serious breeders will never offer stud service to an unregistered queen, and many will reject even registered queens of poor quality. You could buy a male kitten, but stud cats require special care and conditions that you may not be prepared for, as well as a regular supply of queens. Besides, if you purchase a breeding pair of unregistered cats, you are probably paying the price of a good registered breeding queen, so why not start off right?

What about the day you have your first litter of non-registered kittens for sale? You'll quickly learn to make excuses. The buyer may not care if the kitten itself has papers, but he *will* want to be assured that it is a purebred. Registration of the parents is his guarantee. So why aren't the parents registered? Well, this man was going to send me the papers but he left town and I can't get hold of him... I found this queen wandering out in the snow near a large cattery... the registration papers were burned in a fire... the cat fancy is prejudiced against me and won't issue papers.

Here is a possibility that's rarely considered — until it happens. Even if you're breeding together two cats of mediocre quality, it's possible over the long run that you're going to get a kitten that surpasses either parent in quality, maybe even the sort of dream-kitten that breeders wait years for, a kitten that you feel would be competitive at the shows. What then? You can't show it, since it isn't registered. You can't sell it for any more than your other kittens, for the same reason. You can keep it, but its progeny won't be worth any more than other non-registered kittens, and if it's a male, its stud value will be nil.

Don't be deceived into thinking that you can upgrade the progeny of pet queens to show-quality status. It would require many years and generations to do so, if you could manage it at all. Why throw away decades of other people's work by trying to start from scratch? Certainly you could breed Himalayans from Siamese and Persians as was done fifty years ago, but why would you want to when good, registered kittens are readily available? It's false economy to spend a lot of time in an effort to save a little money. If your eventual goal is to breed show kittens, you'll never get there with unregistered cats. Go ahead and breed a litter from your pet if you must, but begin right now to look for a good registered breeding or show quality kitten.

Part of what you pay for when you buy a cat for breeding is the breeder's advice. The breeder of non-registered cats is more likely to be from the "throw 'em together and see what comes out" school; she sells you a kitten and hopes never to hear from you again. But when you buy from a serious breeder, she makes available to you all her knowledge and experience — an asset that can easily be worth hundreds of dollars and may save you years of frustration and wasted time.

Choose cats from good bloodlines

Many of the breeder's potential customers will have seen a cat of the chosen breed at a show, owned one previously, or seen photos in a cat encyclopedia. They will have certain expectations of what the kitten should look like when it grows up. If those expectations are not fulfilled they will be disappointed in their pet and feel unfairly treated by the breeder. The pet buyer will simply not understand that what is sold as a "Himalayan" can vary from a rangy colorpoint with a little extra coat to the long-haired, cobby, snub-nosed cats seen at the shows, and everything in between. He may not realize until the kitten grows up that it is not what he expected. In selling a kitten as a member of a breed, the breeder makes a promise to the buyer — perhaps unspoken, but a promise nonetheless — that that kitten will grow up to be a good representative of its breed.

It costs little more to start with excellent stock than with substandard animals. Over its lifetime a cat will cost around $1800 in food and health care — more for a cat used in breeding and showing — and the cost is the same regardless of the quality of the animal. The difference in *total* cost of buying and keeping a top-quality cat is really small, proportionately. And remember that a registered breeding-quality queen from good stock will repay her purchase cost with her first litter or two.

Choosing a breed

Besides your personal preferences, the main concern in choosing a breed is the market for your kittens. If you plan on having a multitude of kittens of a less popular breed you could have trouble selling all the kittens to good homes. The breeder with just a few cats need not worry, for there will be a market, however small, for just about anything. Even such breeds as the Sphinx (hairless cat) will have a few advocates: those who like to startle visitors and collectors of the rare.

If you choose a less-popular breed, you may have to work doubly hard at the shows and when selling your kittens, for you will have to create interest in the breed. On the other hand, you may have more demand than you can possibly fill from out-of-area buyers, especially right after an article on your breed appears in one of the national magazines.

In choosing a breed, do not be misled by descriptions such as "affectionate, very intelligent, healthy, good temperament" and so forth. Cats differ *individually* in these respects, but not as an entire breed. The only general distinction that can be made between breeds (outside of appearance, of course) is that the shorthair cats tend to be more vocal and more active; the longhairs are quieter and gentler. This distinction is generally true of domestic cats as well as purebreds. Anything else you hear concerning temperament or intelligence should be taken with a grain of salt.

Another distinction between breeds that you're likely to hear is that some are *natural* and others are *man-made*. Breeders of such cats as the Manx and Siamese, whose distinguishing characteristics are of great antiquity, are especially fond of touting their breeds as natural, leaving the novice with the impression that the so-called man-made breeds were synthesized from petrochemicals and popped out of a laboratory test-tube. This distinction is utter nonsense. No doubt the Himalayan would be called a "natural" breed if its founders had searched for longhair colorpoints in free-breeding cat populations (where they could certainly have found them) or waited for one to crop up in a litter of kittens. Instead they followed the sensible course of breeding Persians with Siamese, earning for their breed the dubious distinction of being "man-made." A little thought will reveal that *all* breeds are man-made in exactly the same degree, for in the very process of selection we are preempting the *natural* course that breeding would otherwise follow. If we want to create a truly natural breed we will open the cattery door and allow our queens to mate with whatever toms chance — or nature — sends our way. The only *natural* breed is the non-breed: the domestic.

Creating a new breed

Working towards a new breed, exciting as the prospect may be, should not be considered until you have bred, shown and worked with one or more of the traditional breeds for many years. You should know exactly what you're getting into in terms of time, money and frustration.

You must make every effort to discover if someone else has already been working in the same direction. You should contact a geneticist at a nearby zoo or university and interest him in your project. Above all, you must catch the interest of other breeders and persuade them to devote some of their resources to the new breed, for without widespread appeal a new breed has no chance of being recognized or perpetuating itself.

Specializing in a color

Your chosen breed may be one in which no color variety is possible, but the great majority of breeds offer many different colors and patterns, and more are being accepted yearly by the associations. If you decide to breed Persians, for example, you will almost certainly want to choose a particular division of that breed; for example, the solids, the bicolors, or the shaded. You may want to specialize even further within the division.

The novice breeder inevitably wants to produce a variety of colors. What could be more boring than the same old color, litter after litter? I was no exception. In the course of learning cat color genetics, I even figured out a single mating that could result in over forty different colors. It was purely theoretical. The cats required did not exist, but could certainly have been produced if all one wanted was the greatest range of colors possible.

The wise breeder does just the opposite, and specializes in one color or color group. In Persians, for example, the color-bred blue (product of generations of blue to blue breedings) is a very different color than the blue produced by chance from black, red and tortoiseshell breedings. But the best creams are usually *not* the result of cream-to-cream matings. There are many different shades of every color, including white and black, and it can take years to discover how to produce the best shade of a single color. Finally, the use of certain colors and patterns may be detrimental to other colors and patterns. The more you can specialize, the faster you will learn and the greater your chance of success.

Second breeds

A few people have the idea of starting out with two or more different breeds. This would be most unwise. Unless you choose breeds that can be interbred, a second breed can be accommodated only at the expense of the first. Difficulties in cattery management multiply. Really learning about just *one* breed can take many, many years. The novice breeder should gain plenty of experience before even considering a second breed.

Buying your first cat

Your first step after choosing a breed will be to locate a breeder. Your goal is not merely to make your first purchase, but to make contact within the breed circle and establish a source of information about the breed. This can be one of the most difficult hurdles in your career as a cat breeder. You are not only looking for someone in the breed you've chosen, but someone who shows competitively, has healthy breeding stock, is in your area, is prepared to sell to novices, and is willing to share her knowledge.

You should immediately subscribe to one of the major cat magazines. These will supply you with a nation-wide show calender, show results, articles on feline health and nutrition and extensive advertising of cat-related products and catteries. These magazines can be found at most pet shops, at shows, or write to the addresses in the back of this book.

Look through the magazine for the address of a breeder near you. If you don't find one listed in your area, call any of the breeders listed and ask her how you can find a breeder in your state. Call, don't write – many breeders will not respond to written requests for "information;" they get so many of these.

Once you've found a local breeder, try to arrange a visit even if there are no kittens for sale at the moment. Ask questions about the breed and the breeder's bloodlines, and try to establish yourself as a person sincerely interested in breeding cats.

Some breeders will try to discourage you, making you wonder exactly why they are advertising. Simple: they must sell their pet kittens and they advertise to generate *pet* sales and sales to established breeders. They are wary of anyone new entering the breed.

Use the magazine's show calendar to note any upcoming shows in your area. Until you are actively involved in the cat fancy, the show calendar could be your only way of locating shows. A few shows get considerable revenue from admitting the public and are given lots of publicity, but most are not advertised at all.

The magazine's show calendar will give the entry clerk's address. Write to her, enclosing a stamped, self-addressed envelope. The entry form she sends back will give you the location of the show. By all means send in an entry if you have a showable cat (altered domestics can be shown as household pets). Once you start showing you'll be placed on cat clubs' mailing lists to receive entry forms for future shows. If you don't have a cat to show, call the entry clerk for the show location.

At the show, look for entries in your chosen breed and talk to the owners. Look for cattery cards and exhibitors' lists in the back of the show catalog, so you can call after the show when the exhibitor is not so busy.

Veterinary clinics are a good bet for locating breeders or finding out about upcoming shows. And if you locate a large-scale breeder who is active in showing, even in another breed, give her a call. She will probably know people in your breed.

The great majority of breeders do not advertise in the national magazines or anywhere else except when they have surplus pet kittens for sale, and then they will advertise in the classified section of a local newspaper. Check regularly for ads and call everyone who advertises your breed. These ads may be placed by people who have just one queen they breed occasionally. If so, try to get the name and number of the stud's owner. Every litter must have a sire, and those people who keep registered toms at stud are likely to be just the ones you're looking for. And so much the better if you make contact with a stud owner, since you will be needing stud service in the near future.

Another way to locate breeders is through the publications put out by breed and cat associations. These are often advertised in the cat magazines.

It's wise to shop around for bloodlines you like, but don't wait too long to buy your first purebred kitten. The best way to learn about a breed is to show and breed a cat of that breed, whether or not that cat's bloodlines are those you finally decide to stay with. It will take at least a year or two of showing and studying the breed to decide just who has cats with the look you like best. Even a year is not really long enough, because some breeders working for the long-term will not show every season.

Almost everyone wants to start with the best possible cats from winning bloodlines, but there are several factors working against the novice. Your first goal, therefore, should be to purchase a breeding-quality queen (that you can still show, though she would not be expected to win) from a local breeder who can serve as your entry into the breed circle.

Caveat Emptor

The old rule was never so true. People are often spendthrift when it comes to their hobbies: they pinch every penny at the supermarket, but they fork over hundreds of dollars for kittens and cats of dubious merit without a second thought. Anyone starting out in cats who broadcasts the word that she "wants to start with the best — price is no object" is asking for trouble.

It's not so much that breeders are dishonest — though a few are. The problem is that many breeders are cattery-blind. They are so used to the look of their own cats that they're unable to judge how a kitten might do at the shows in relation to someone else's entry.

Breeders are well aware of the three arbitrary divisions by which price is determined: pet, breeder, and show quality. They automatically divide their own kittens into these divisions when they prepare to sell them. The best one or two out of a dozen will be labelled show quality, the middle ones breeding quality, and the remainder pets. If most of the kittens are mediocre, the one best kitten can start to look very good indeed. But once that kitten gets to the shows, the woeful truth may become evident: while the kitten looked great next to its brothers and sisters, it's mediocre compared to the other kittens being shown. How was the breeder to know? In any case, she has a safe way out: she can always say the kitten had great potential but didn't turn out as well as expected.

Also not to be underrated is the lure of the fast buck. When a kitten customer walks in the door with a roll of hundreds outstretched, breeding-quality kittens can bloom instantaneously into top show prospects.

Then there are the breeders who *underrate* their kittens in their desire to give true value for dollars paid. The breeding kitten they sell you for $500 will win easily over the $1500 show prospect sold to you by the first breeder.

If you are not yet a good judge of merit in your breed, it will be impossible to tell which is which. For this reason, I'm going to go against the traditional maxim to "buy the very best you can afford" when starting out, and advise you to buy a good-quality breeding kitten and show it for a season, taking every opportunity to study the winning cats of your breed, learning to develop an eye for a real winner, and finding out who charges fair prices and who doesn't; *then* go out and buy your show-quality kittens. There's no shame in showing a breeding-quality cat if that's all you've got to show; almost everyone starts that way. And there's always a chance that the kitten you pay $500 for as a breeder could be the very same one you'd have paid a lot more for if you'd asked for a show kitten!

If you're really determined to start out at the top there are a few ways to attempt it. First, buy a kitten at or after a show if you see one you like. The price is not likely to be inflated and you'll be able to see exactly how well it does. Second, you could enlist the help of an exhibitor-breeder in a different, but related, breed, or of a judge, for his assistance in locating a show-quality kitten of the breed you want, possibly for a finder's fee.

Remember when you begin showing that shows differ widely in the caliber of cats they attract: you might hit one at which half the big guns in the country decide to fly in for the weekend, in which case even a top-flight kitten might not be a finals winner. The converse, of course, is also true: you may overrate a kitten's merit if it's showing against cats of little quality. Take your kitten to a sampling of shows and don't hesitate to ask other breeders what they think of its qualities before you decide to either give up or to go national with it!

Thinking back over my own purchases, it's evident that the connection between price and quality has been tenuous. My most expensive cat did nothing at the shows and produced nothing at home, while my bargain-basement special — a kitten I bought for her superior bloodlines and not for her looks — has produced my finest kittens.

The prejudice against the novice breeder

Bear this in mind when you're looking for your first show kitten: the novice who is able to buy a *really* top kitten *at any price whatsoever* is lucky indeed. Breeders want to sell their best kittens to other breeders, not to beginners.

From the standpoint of the established breeder, the novice breeder might represent unwanted competition. Many experienced breeders have a longstanding, though friendly, feud as to who has the best cats. How will they regard the newcomer to the show ring? They'll pity her if she loses, and despise her if she wins. It isn't *fair* for a newcomer to win; the ribbons should go to those who've been through many losing cats, cattery problems and accumulating debts; in other words, those who've suffered.

I've often heard a novice exhibitor say that she showed her cat in three or four shows and not a single exhibitor would say a word to her. Some breeders seem to think the beginner should serve a long apprenticeship before being allowed into the magic circle. I find this attitude annoying. The cat fancy, to remain active, must be continually attracting new devotees.

On the other hand, the experienced breeders have seen many people start out in the breed and give it up after a year or so. And most breeders don't want to sell their best kitten locally. If they do, it will be competing with her own cats. The serious breeder has worked long and hard on establishing her line and she may not want to sell a cat for breeding to someone whose goals and attitudes are entirely unknown. I know of a breeder who turned downed an offer of $2500 for a kitten and then sold it for $800 to someone else because she thought the second person would show it better. Breeders' motivations are not always monetary.

Many serious breeders have helped newcomers to the breed, only to find their time wasted on people who were not really interested. It's the best-known story in the cat fancy: the show-quality kitten that was sold to the novice breeder who promised to show it and never did – what a terrible waste! If you stay in the cat fancy long enough, I can guarantee that it will happen to you, too.

Buying out of the area

Breeders like to sell good kittens out of the area because they are removing local competition and promoting their own cattery in another part of the country.

However, the buyer should be careful of buying a kitten sight unseen. Many people, including experienced breeders, have purchased show quality kittens that dwindled to pet quality somewhere between airports.

If you buy a kitten sight-unseen, even if you've seen photos of it, work out a clear return agreement. If the breeder cavils at the suggestion, be suspicious. Everyone will claim they're not in cat breeding for the money, and in general, that's true. But if nobody's in it for the money, why are so many people getting ripped off?

Remember, too, when you're buying a kitten from out of the area, that it will be costly to communicate with the breeder. Every novice should buy at least *one* kitten locally to take advantage of a near-by breeder's expertise and contacts.

Ultimately, the best rule for the purchaser is this: buy your cats from people you like, people who seem fair and will approach any dealings with you in a businesslike manner. Forget the others. They may be producing some terrific cats, but your chances of getting a square deal from them are slim indeed.

Most cat breeders are straightforward, honest people. But don't assume too much from the fact that you both love cats.

Learning about your chosen breed

When you buy your first kitten, ask the breeder about books, magazines and clubs involved with your breed. Magazines and club newsletters are particularly useful in gathering specific information about bloodlines, pedigrees, color genetics and experimental work pertaining to your breed alone. Advertising in such periodicals is usually very cheap and is a good way to get nation-wide exposure for your cattery name. There is hardly a breed of cat, however new or small, that does not have a breed club and periodical literature; the more popular breeds have several clubs as well as independent magazines.

Pet shops

Buying a kitten for breeding from a pet shop is not advisable. First, you're going to pay a much higher price than you would from a breeder. Pet shops don't usually breed their own kittens; they buy from local breeders or commercial catteries. Those breeders willing to sell through retail outlets are held in disrepute by most serious breeders. Too often they are interested in easy money and care not a whit who buys their kittens. Although a pet shop owner may assure you that such-and-such a kitten is of "breeding quality" or "good enough to show," chances are he knows little of the breed and nothing of the breeder. The kittens may have been shipped hundreds of miles. They may have been raised in deplorable conditions and roughly handled. Invariably they are taken from their mothers far too soon, for it takes time to ship and sell them, and they've got to be sold before the cute stage is over. Early kittenhood is comparable in every way to a human's childhood, and proper socialization and the freedom to explore and become accustomed to humans and households are of the utmost importance. The pet shop kitten misses it all. Many pet shop owners don't sell puppies or kittens for the same reason – they are animal lovers, too. They may have listings of breeders in the area, however.

Selling your kittens through pet shops should be eschewed for the same reasons. Some breed associations have a code of ethics that disqualifies members who are known to sell through pet shops.

The entire male

The tom is the subject of many mysteries to the novice breeder, who is sure to hear him maligned. Some breeders will tell you that you should have *x* years experience with cats before owning a tom. But lots of people own toms, not just breeders. Some have lived with a tom for years on end without even knowing "her" true sex.

The worst crime of the tom is probably his habit of spraying urine on everything around him. Many toms, however, *never* spray. Indoor/outdoor toms may spray outside, where they can scent strangers, but not indoors. Others may not begin spraying until introduced to a new home or a strange cat. There's nothing the tom's owner can do to control spraying: either you're lucky or you're not. My guess is that as many toms do *not* spray as those that do. Some queens also spray, especially when in estrus.

If you're buying a tom, don't depend on luck. Build special accommodations for the young male and accustom him to them from an early age. Even if he never starts spraying, you'll still have a good breeding cage/isolation unit/maternity ward. Separate cat quarters never go to waste!

Even if your tom confines himself to a litter box, he will still make his presence known through the pungent odor of his urine. Be sure his quarters are in an airy, easy-to-clean room or outdoors. Most cats, given a choice, will use a box outdoors rather than indoors, so an outdoor run attached to the house would be ideal for those who also want to give their toms the run of the house.

Is it true that males must have a certain number of females to keep them happy? Will they become vicious and hard to handle if deprived? Certainly toms *are* more settled when allowed to breed frequently or live with their own harem. But there are few toms anywhere provided with a queen every week, which some authorities advocate. There are toms lucky to see a queen every three months that seem hardly the worse for it. Of course, you must not accustom a tom to frequent use and then suddenly take away his queens. A tom so deprived, or a tom bred infrequently, should be neutered and, if necessary, given away as a pet.

For most breeders, it is just not practical to have a dozen queens per tom. Three or four is probably the average, and will keep the tom quite content.

Give the young male plenty of handling, grooming and bathing when he is young and he'll never be hard to handle. Give him sweet-tempered mates for his first few breedings, if possible.

A cryptorchid is a male whose testicles have not descended: such a cat is infertile. A unilateral cryptorchid or monorchid is a male with only one testicle; this does not impair fertility, and monorchids can be shown in some associations. But many breeders would not accept a monorchid into a breeding program, since the condition is thought to be hereditary, predisposes the hidden testicle to cancer, and is also believed to accompany an uncertain temperament. The pet buyer also loses out when he buys a cryptorchid or monorchid kitten, because the vet must search through the cat's abdomen for the testicles when neutering: a time-consuming and costly task.

It's surprising how many people buy a male for breeding without concerning themselves with that which makes it possible for him to breed. You should check the kitten's apparatus before buying (and also check the male kittens you sell). The testicles are occasionally discernable at birth and almost always present at about three months' age — the age at which most kittens are sold. If they have not descended by six months' age they probably will never do so, though there have been exceptions. If the tom's potential stud value is very high, it might be possible to surgically lower the testicles, depending on their position.

Continue to arrange stud service for your queens even after buying your male kitten, since he may mature very slowly.

Buy your tom when you can find a good one and don't be scared off by breeders who say that novice breeders shouldn't keep toms — after all, by the time he's grown up and sired a few litters, you won't be a novice any more. If your breed is an unusual one or if no studs are readily available to you, you'll have no choice but to keep a tom at stud. In such a situation you might consider a co-ownership agreement with others with queens of your breed to offset some of the purchase price and upkeep.

Buying mature cats for breeding

Buying a proven breeding queen from good bloodlines is an excellent way to start in cats. First, you will be able to breed her at once, whereas with a kitten you must wait for her to mature. Second, you have the assurance that the queen is fertile, a willing breeder, carries her kittens to term and mothers them successfully: all unknowns when you buy a kitten. Third, you can expect to get a very good price, since the vast majority of people want kittens.

But be careful. Why is this female for sale? Is she difficult to breed? Has few kittens? A poor mother? Ask a lot of questions or you could buy a lot of problems.

The novice is advised to purchase his *males* while they are still kittens (under eight months). If an older tom is being considered, some precautions should be taken. Most males are intensely territorial: they will not mate anywhere and everywhere. When the tom is moved to strange ground, there's a strong possibility that his breeding performance may deteriorate — or vanish altogether until he begins to feel secure in his new environment. If you do decide to buy a mature tom, purchasing a familiar queen at the same time may make him feel more at home. If this is not possible, the tom could be placed with a placid, unthreatening alter or kitten. Certainly no mature tom should be brought into new quarters and immediately thrown together with a lot of strange queens. He must be allowed plenty of time. A guarantee of breeding performance, return privilege, or some other form of protection should be part of the purchase agreement.

Alternate ways to begin in cats

It is possible, from time to time, to purchase in its entirety a large, successful cattery, including breeding stock, equipment, records, and contacts.

It is also possible to purchase cats of the highest caliber, current national winners, to start one's cattery with the very best. If you have plenty of money and you see a winning cat that strikes your fancy, don't wait until you see a For Sale sign. Many of the best cats are available for the right price. You might also try to purchase or breed to the parents of a top show winner, and hope for more of the same.

Another way of starting out would be to lease a good queen long enough to raise a litter from her. Large breeders might not have space or time to breed from every queen, and might be amenable to the idea of leasing.

The novice breeder can sometimes help large breeders by participating in their breeding plan: she might be given a queen in return for two kittens from the same queen at a future date. However, most breeders tend to be wary of leasing or kitten-return agreements unless they already know the person involved: too many such people have vanished, cats and all.

Buying from a small breeder

The large-scale breeder may see a hundred kittens passing through every year. She acquires experience that much faster than the small breeder, so her judgment of a kitten's potential may be more accurate than the small breeder's.

On the other hand, she's unlikely to sell you a really outstanding kitten because she'll keep it herself (with forty cats, what's one more?)

The smaller breeder doesn't advertise nationally and therefore sells most of her kittens locally, as pets. Unless she has built an outstanding reputation — which will take her much longer than the big breeder because she has fewer animals to work with — there may be little demand for her best kittens. The very fact that she is a small breeder shows that she can't keep all her best kittens; moreover, she may be working with exactly the same bloodlines as a big breeder, but because she is not as well known the availability of her kittens may be much better.

Cattery size

First a warning: the greatest mistake the novice can make is to purchase or keep too many cats at the outset. A cat is a living animal, and cannot be set aside or discarded like a stamp collection one's grown tired of.

During the first year or so, you may well have problems in locating breeders and persuading them to sell you good breeding stock. Kittens for sale seem few and far between. But once you begin showing and breeding, the offers may come in thick and fast. It's hard to turn down an excellent prospect, harder still not to keep some kittens from your first few litters, those very first that carry *your* cattery name.

Consider, first, that your initial enthusiasm may wane in a couple of years. Secondly, remember the humans that share your life, who may not be enamoured to a herd of cats. And finally, if you truly wish to establish your own strain, you must bring in outside bloodlines only with care, planning, and great stinginess. If you have faith in your foundation stock and the ultimate success of your breeding plan, do not throw all to the winds for the sake of one cute kitten.

You may see ads in the cat magazines placed by breeders who claim they are "going out of business." This is often a version of the never-ending sale: the ad really means that they have a perpetual sale on adult breeding stock. While it *is* sometimes necessary to sell or give away an adult, a continual overpopulation problem is sure to be the result of poor planning.

My suggestion for the majority of novice breeders: start with one breeding queen (purchased locally if possible), add another when you've found the bloodlines you like and buy a male of the same strain or keep a good male kitten from the queen, unless stud service is readily available. At this point — after about two years of breeding — decide firmly how many cats you must limit yourself to, and stick to it! Remember to leave room for an outstanding kitten or two: it's just when you don't expect much from a particular breeding that the good ones pop up.

If you intend to keep only one or two adult cats, they should be females. With this small a number, you should consider buying a male only if there are no good males readily available at stud in your area. This may well be the case with the rare breeds. If so, you should find out if other breeders would be interested in co-owning a male. Even with a male, however, so small a population cannot be self-sufficient for more than a few years, and therefore makes you dependent on other breeders. There's nothing wrong with this as long as you've found someone you like and can work with; in fact, in can even be a tremendous advantage, for if you have attached yourself to a rising star, your own will rise too at a rate you could probably not achieve on your own.

A more workable number for a self-sufficient cattery is four or five cats, one of them being a male. Here is enough of a "gene pool" to avoid too close inbreeding for at least a couple of generatons.

An excellent number for a small cattery is around eight cats, two males and six females. Cattery management is not too burdensome, your cattery is self-sufficient, and you can actually keep two separate lines going if necessary. This provides you with a place to go if your cats start becoming too inbred.

If more cats are added, keep in mind a general ratio of three or four females to each male.

Chapter Three: *Cattery Management*

Handling cats

Some animals trust humans, either through nature or force of habit, to the extent of obeying them even in circumstances that threaten their own lives.

Cats have a relatively low acceptance level of irritation and discomfort at the hands of humans, at least compared to dogs or horses. However, any cat should submit to such minor annoyances as being bathed, groomed, given a pill, having its temperature taken, or being handled by a vet or show judge. Proper daily handling will reinforce the lessons learned in kittenhood. The breeder should get in the habit of handling all cats correctly, for even if he trusts his own completely, he will, at times, have to handle strange and perhaps aggressive cats.

When removing a cat from a carrier or cage, touch it first in the side or flank area and slide its body so that the cat is facing away from you. Then lift it out backwards.

Carry a cat facing away from you by placing one hand under its rib cage with its body resting along your forearm (a one-arm carry). This position is comfortable to the cat and protective to you, since it keeps the armory facing outwards. Cats at shows are usually carried this way, too, since the coat will be least disturbed. Additional control can be gained by holding the cat under your left arm with the head and shoulders facing backwards and the right hand supporting the hindquarters.

A hand approaching the head, especially from above, is a threatening gesture to almost all animals; so is an "attack" from behind. Reach instead for the neutral middle of the body and approach sideways, especially with very young kittens, who are easily startled.

Use your voice, either to soothe a frightened animal or scold a rowdy one (it's rather hard, however, to intimidate a cat). All cats like to be spoken to. They cannot interpret your facial expressions as another human would, so your tone of voice allows them to gauge your mood. A friendly greeting is the equivalent of a smile. You determine your cat's mood by its expression, its body position and its tail movements.

If a cat is badly injured or panicked, trap it in a blanket or drop a box over it.

Even the gentlest cat can do a lot of damage if it feels cornered or terrified, so use caution.

I think the best way to punish misbehavior is a quick shake and a few stern words followed almost at once by petting and praise if the misbehavior stops. A shake allows you to keep firm control of the cat and tends to frighten it less than a slap. It should never be necessary to strike a cat.

But be sure to distinguish between misbehavior and panic. The frightened cat must be soothed and calmed, not punished. Don't try to hold it if it's really terrified, as restraint may only create more panic.

Proper handling means teaching your cats that they must submit to restraint. Don't free a cat that's struggling to escape. Wait until it is quiet and then place it quietly on the ground. With a little effort you'll teach your cats to stand still to be groomed or bathed without complaint.

When handling an obstinate cat, try straddling its body and "sitting" on it to control it when giving a pill or taking its temperature.

Injuries from cats

Most scratches just need to be cleaned, and perhaps an antiseptic applied. Bite wounds from cats, while they may be almost invisible, are much more serious. They look like tiny punctures and may bleed very little, but the chance of infection is great. Bites can cause numbness, swelling, and aching pain. A tetanus shot and a course of antibiotics might be advised by your doctor. Should the cat belong to another person, inform the owner at once so the cat can be watched for any sign of rabies (a very remote possibility in a purebred cat).

In a lifetime spent with animals, I have been bitten only once, by a cat not my own. I am never scratched, even in play, except by very young kittens who have not yet learned to respect human flesh. All cats that have been gently raised and frequently handled will submit with good grace to proper handling.

Choosing a veterinarian

Veterinarians often have little empathy with cat breeders because of their orientation to correcting the overpopulation problem by spaying and neutering, while the breeders, from their point of view, keep adding to it. They tend to debunk the special status of the purebred. Many object to some breeders' practice of giving their own vaccinations and simple medications without professional assitance. But other veterinarians are more than willing to help the breeder, and a few even get tired of vaccinating litter after litter and insist on showing the breeder how to do it herself.

The breeder, on the other hand, can develop an unfortunate antipathy towards veterinarians in general, perhaps because veterinarians become accustomed to very simplified explanations or advice suitable for pet owners but annoying to the serious breeder who, after all, has a professional outlook too.

The breeder should try to find a veterinarian she trusts, and in particular one who is not averse to late-night emergency calls or answering questions occasionally over the phone to a well-established client. A vet who specializes in cats – usually found in larger cities only – is highly recommended. Every breeder should take full advantage of a veterinarian's extensive training, not just when she has problems, but as an aid in preventing problems.

For assistance in the mechanical aspects of breeding and kittening, however, call an experienced breeder. Cat breeders become specialists and gain more experience over the years in the practical aspects of breeding and kittening than the vast majority of vets.

On caging

Many novices regard the idea of caging cats with horror. But consider: there are many types of cages. Some are tiny show-sized units stacked floor to ceiling in a dingy basement. Others are heated, air-conditioned, well furnished with shelves and toys and beds, have piped-in music and spacious outdoor runs attached, lots of activity to watch and a buddy or two to play with. Is a cat that lives in such a cage worse off than the one that shares an entire house with dozens of other cats?

Almost anyone who breeds cats will find that he needs compartments, whether they are rooms or cages, to isolate sick cats or incoming cats that may carry infection, for a maternity ward, to separate males and females during the breeding season, to prevent the stud from spraying all over the house, and so forth. Occasional caging does no harm, nor does permanent caging if it's suited to the cat's needs.

The first cattery I ever visited was owned by a couple living in a small apartment, very proud of the fact that they didn't cage their cats. There were so many cats that I hardly had anywhere to put my feet, and when I lifted one off a chair so I could sit down, another immediately filled the gap. The second cattery I visited was in a house. There were only two cats in the living room when I entered, and I wondered why this woman was supposed to be such a big breeder. I found out when we went downstairs: a hundred tiny cages, each containing one cat, one water dish and one tiny litter box – there was no room for more. It was obvious that those cats spent their entire lives in a space hardly twice the length of their bodies. Surely this sort of caging is what people have in mind when they protest that cats should never be caged.

On having cats put down

The cat, like all animals, lives in the present. It has no sense of past or future, and thus none of the fears — or hopes — that belong to the human race. When an animal suffers, it suffers more than a person because it has no knowledge that it can recover: suffering becomes its entire being. All animals must die, but they need not suffer.

I approach this subject because of the pain I myself have gone through with terminal illnesses in cats. The reputed "nine lives" of cats is a tribute more to their agility than to their health. Cats do poorly in a prolonged illness. Many endure terrible pain, surgery, and hospitalization because their owners hope they might recover: three of these cats were mine, and all died in the end. In future, hard though it may be to do so, I intend to take my vet's advice, and if a cat has little chance of recovery have it put gently to sleep rather than end its life in agony.

After all, we who breed and care for cats are playing god in a small way, and we should not shirk the responsibility of determining the end for our pets.

The handicapped cat or kitten, however, should not be destroyed without some thought as to whether or not a good home can be found for it. Many deaf cats are kept by people who don't even know their cat is handicapped. And there are plenty of people who will love a handicapped kitten all the more, just as they might a handicapped child. Kittens that are born blind or have missing limbs can still lead happy, healthy lives; in fact, unlike a human child, they will never even be aware of their handicap.

Shipping a cat

Cats can be inexpensively shipped as air freight to almost any point in the United States and overseas. Current rates for coast-to-coast air shipment are around $90.00.

The person shipping the cat must arrange for an approved carrier. Carriers can be purchased from many, but not all, airlines, and from pet stores — but be sure you know the regulations first if you don't buy directly from the airline. Arrange as direct a flight as possible to the airport where the cat will be picked up since problems, when they occur, are most likely to be failed transfers. The shipper should ask about insurance — there may be an amount to which all cargo is automatically insured — and find out from the purchaser whether or not she wishes additional insurance (the cat belongs to the purchaser as soon as the seller releases it to the airline). The cost of shipping, but not of the carrier, is payable at either end. Normally, the person purchasing the cat or sending it to be bred will pay for the shipping. If sent COD, the sender must guarantee payment for care and return of cats that are shipped and then stranded. If this happens, the airline must call the sender and return the cat within forty-eight hours of this notice. The airline is also required to furnish a sanitary holding area with fresh air and controlled temperature for all animals.

The shipper must inform the receiver of when to expect the cat, and arrange for a final call when the cat is on its way.

Current regulations require that kittens be at least eight weeks old before shipping, and be fully weaned at least five days prior to shipping. Most breeders have more strict requirements, and would not want to ship a kitten until it is from twelve to sixteen weeks old. Cats in early pregnancy can be safely shipped — in fact, a cat shipped away from home for breeding should stay with the stud's owner until it is determined that she is pregnant (about three weeks) because of the time and expense involved in shipping.

In general, cats should not be tranquillized before being shipped. Cats react erratically to the same dosage and type of tranquillizer, and what puts one cat into a doze can send another into hysterics. Cats will require a certificate of health signed by a licensed veterinarian within ten days before shipping.

The sender can tape full information as to the addresses of sender and receiver to the inside of the carrier, since if the cat is lost it can hardly be expected to speak for itself. Pedigrees and registration certificates can also be placed in an envelope and taped to the inside of the carrier.

The receiver should make a careful note of the place of shipment, transfer points, flight number, carrier and arrival time. She should take with her the sender's phone number in case verification of shipping should be necessary. A clean carrier might also come in useful if the cat has soiled its own.

Few shipments go astray, and when they do, the cat almost always arrives safely, though bedraggled from a long journey. Shipping kittens and cats is a routine matter for many breeders.

Be sure to check the airline's regulations as to temperature. Although the airline provides a pressurized, climate-controlled area for pets shipped as cargo, they are concerned with the time spent on the runway while the plane is loaded and unloaded. If temperatures at departure or arrival cities or any transfer cities in between do not fall within the acceptable range, the airline will refuse to accept the cat. In some cases the sender can sign a waiver (for example, for a longhair cat used to outdoor temperatures). In other cases, they will simply refuse to accept the shipment. I have waited through most of one summer to ship a cat because of these restrictions. I have also made several middle-of-the-night trips to airports only to discover that the temperature had dropped, or risen, in the arrival city.

Of course, if you can take the cat yourself as a "carry-on," such restrictions do not apply, and the cat accompanies you in the passenger compartment. It will need a health certificate and a carrier that will fit under the seat, and you'll have to pay an extra fee, usually $30 each way. The airline also usually limits cats in the passenger area to one, so you need to "reserve" this space in advance. So few people takes pets on planes that this is seldom a problem. Show campaigners who fly regularly with their cats sometimes do not declare them to save paying the extra fee.

The economics of breeding

Few people can make a living breeding cats. Breeders create a product that's in demand, but supply is also high. Just about anyone can breed cats: at the most basic level, it requires no special facilities, no expertise, and small investment. Certainly many people have found themselves cat breeders by accident and regretted the fact.

The cat breeder's prices are restricted to some degree by the oversupply of kittens. She sells, of course, to a different market. Still, the prospective buyer knows that free kittens are readily available, and many people scoff at the very idea of paying money for a mere cat.

The market for the superstar kittens is limited to other show breeders and exhibitors. You are not going to attract the attention of such people for many years, and only then if you've had great success. As a novice, your primary market will be pet kittens, and these will sell for whatever the going rate is for your breed and area, perhaps $175 or so. Aha, you think, can't I still make money at $175 per kitten?

Well, you could — if you cut corners everywhere, often to the detriment of your cats. On the other hand, the moans and groans you hear from so many breeders that they are losing money left and right in their cat hobby are usually exaggerated. No one needs to be rich to subsidize a cat breeding hobby. In fact, after a year or two of setting up, during which you will have to pay for foundation stock and facilities, you should expect to break even or make a small profit from your cats. If you don't, either you don't care about the money or you enjoy moaning and groaning.

Keeping your costs down

Here are some tips for saving money without compromising on the quality of your breeding stock or on their welfare, while remaining fair with your customers.

Your first large expense is breeding stock. You can save a bundle if you're patient and can resist the temptation of cuddly kittens (you'll have plenty of kittens around soon enough, anyway!). Buy an older breeding queen. Most breeders have to occasionally place older breeding stock to make way for new. Some of these "older" queens are really still in their prime: four or five years old. Moreover, they are proven producers, and you can examine their breeding record and perhaps some of the kittens they've produced before you buy. You should not have to pay any more for an older queen than you would for a kitten of equivalent quality, and often you will pay much less. The queen will be ready to breed, whereas a kitten will require eight to twelve month's growth before she will breed. And with a mature queen, what you see is what you get. Many people have paid high prices for kittens with great "potential" that didn't quite live up to it.

It's also possible to get a breeding queen for *nothing,* provided you are willing to leave the cat in the breeder's name and share with her your first litter or two. Breeders often require one or two kittens from a particular cat for their breeding program, but lack of space requires them to sell. However, one would have to know a breeder well before she would accept such an arrangement.

If you are buying stud service, don't try to economize here. The only way you can increase the quality and value of your kittens is by using the very best stud available to you.

In addition, you must never turn down the purchase of an exceptional kitten or cat for monetary reasons. The top quality kittens are so few and far between that you can consider yourself lucky if you are *ever* offered one for sale, whatever the price. Mortgage the house (again) if you have to.

And speaking of housing: the obvious economy is to share your own. Anyone with a few rooms can accommodate cats. When the time comes to build special cat territories, call and visit other cat breeders in the area to see if you can buy used equipment, or you can make your own. This goes, too, for cat furniture and cat trees. Even the all-thumbs builder can usually manage get the right end of the nail in the board. Remember, the cats don't care what their furniture looks like.

On feeding: many generations of laboratory cats have been raised on commercial cat foods. Why do yours need ground sirloin every night? Many breeders have recipes for their cats that would make a Cordon Bleu chef blanch with envy, but if you'll ask around you'll find there are others who feed primarily commercial foods, and their cats do just as well in the show ring and maternity ward. Commercial food and litter can be bought in quantity at warehouse co-ops for two-thirds the supermarket price.

Investigate pet specialty markets and butcher shops for inexpensive meat mixes that can be used as extenders for commercial foods.

Vet bills are going to be the killer. I'm not saying that vets overcharge (they're extremely touchy on the subject, so don't you say it either), but those bills sure do mount up, even *without* any major health problems in your cattery. Call around for comparative rates on simple procedures such as vaccinations and altering. I've found rates to vary from $13 to $35 on the former, $25 to $85 on the latter — an enormous range when you multiply it by several kittens or cats. Learn all you can about cat care; some visits to the vet may be unnecessary. Take full advantage of every visit to your vet: ask questions about vaccines, kittening, injuries – whatever questions you've stored up. Finally, consider ordering your own vaccines, medications and basic cat-care products from mail-order supply houses.

The best economy in health care is preventive care.

Advertising and promotion can be a big expense, but you must find buyers for your kittens. Many veterinarians have bulletin boards where you can put your card up. Make sure you are listed as a breeder at the pet shops you patronize.

Your greatest savings here can be to take full advantage of every show you attend to attract kitten buyers. Find out which shows attract the greatest number of exhibitors, and print up cattery cards and information sheets on your breed to hand out to interested people. Even if you won't have any kittens for months, you can make enough contacts at a big show to sell several later. I have had people call me for kittens that picked up my card at shows three and four years back!

If you *do* have kittens available, ask the entry clerk about selling them at the show; "For Sale" cages are almost always available for a small fee. Usually the association has some age limitation, i.e., 4 months (CFA, ACFA), or 12 weeks (TICA) on kittens in the show hall. Four months is quite a large kitten; this is longer than most breeders will want to hold a pet. You'll probably see kittens much younger than this for sale at the shows. Never mind; they probably belong to the show manager or her best friend. Don't *you* try it, and if your kittens are unusually small, bring their litter registration as proof of their birthdate.

Word of mouth advertising is also free, and if you develop a reputation for selling healthy, problem-free kittens you'll eventually find that you seldom have to advertise at all, even to sell your pets.

The cattery

For most small breeders, the cattery is their house or apartment. This can mean one or two rooms devoted exclusively to the cats where they spend the majority of their time. You might also consider adding on to your house, building a cattery unit separate from your house, or purchasing a trailer.

Outdoor runs can be built as a supplement to indoor space and will be greatly enjoyed by all cats. In mild climates, cats can live year-round in outdoor cages if shelter from wind and rain is provided. A walk-in run of about 80 square feet can accommodate two or three cats as permanent quarters and provide a part-time run for several. Kennel runs make excellent outdoor cages and can be purchased in various sizes as a kit, or you can build one yourself. Small-gauge chicken wire is sufficient to keep cats in, but you may also be concerned with keeping children and dogs *out,* in which case you'll want to use a strong gauge of steel mesh. Young kittens can walk right though some mesh fences, so add a strip of chicken wire around the bottom. Cats can also climb right up wire mesh, so you must put a ceiling on outdoor caging. This is easily constructed of chicken wire. Gates should lock securely. Furniture should include shelves as well as a cat house and a spot where water and food will not be contaminated. The litter box will also have to be covered (you can buy one with a self-cover); place the box up on bricks for easy cleaning underneath.

Outdoor caging is almost imperative for toms, especially if they are sprayers. However, the tom can make do with a room that is easy to clean and air out. Contrary to common belief, two or three males can usually be kept together (particularly if they have grown up together) as long as queens in heat are not also present.

Cattery walls and floors should be painted or varnished for easy cleaning, or you can use plastic or ceramic tiles. There should be plenty of space for exercising and, if possible, access to an outdoor run. Runs can be shared on a staggered basis by many cats.

Remember when you're planning space that vertical space is just as important as horizontal: cats love jumping and climbing. Each cattery unit should have plenty of room for shelves, a litter box, a scratching post, and feed dishes as well as comfortable sleeping quarters. Easily washable rugs and pillows will help make the cats comfortable.

Every cat should spend part of each day with other cats in your house or a large communal outdoor run. A really excellent setup would consist of large walk-in cages with small individual outdoor runs, encircling a large main run where many cats can be put out togeter.

You must also consider breedng and kittening quarters. For breeding to outside queens, the tom and queen should have a chance to get to know each other through adjacent cages, or the queen can be put in a smaller cage inside the male's quarters. The breeding cage should be large enough for the cats to get away from each other, and should not be close enough to other toms to cause a ruckus. You can, of course, just let the tom run free with your own females, though this has disadvantages: you may not know *when* or even *if* mating has occurred, and will have no way of determining when the kittens are due.

Kittening requires especially warm, clean and accessible areas. Most breeders will use their bedrooms or adjoining rooms so that they will be at hand quickly when kittening starts. If you have several queens, they may each need separate quarters, though many will help each other and share nursing and grooming chores.

Isolation cages will be necessary for new cats coming into the cattery or for sick cats. The isolation unit should be as far away as possible from your main cattery. It should be easy to clean, though it need not be large, since sick cats do not exercise much. Do not interchange feed and water bowls or other furnishings from an isolation unit with those from the main cattery. Diseases can be transmitted from your skin or clothes, so wash thoroughly after handling an infected cat. Only the smallest catteries will not need isolation quarters.

Your cattery planning should take into account convenience of location, availabiltiy of water and electricity, and ease of maintenance. You'll need places for bags of cat litter, extra boxes, carriers, disinfectants, and cat food. A plastic garbage can with a big grain scoop is ideal for cat litter and dry food, which can be dumped into it when purchased and scooped out as necessary. A nearby sink for washing up, sponges, brushes, and so forth, will be needed. Don't forget convenient disposal of used cat litter. If you're not careful with this, your garbage collectors may mutiny. Outdoor ligthing will be a plus for detached and outdoor catteries.

Added conveniences: a radio (for both cats and yourself), a small refrigerator, a grooming table. Consider also having an area where you – and prospective buyers – can sit comfortably to enjoy the cats. Make your cattery clean and attractive, and remember that visitors may want to visit it.

Effective flea control

Fleas are the major parasite problem in all catteries. Almost every cattery of long standing with more than a few cats has occasional flea problems, and many breeders must be content to keep the flea population under control, since it's difficult to completely eradicate it. In states like Florida, because of the climate, eradication is close to impossible.

You may rarely see a flea on your cat but you may see signs: small curling brown specks, which are called flea dirt (flea excrement). These will leave a reddish smear when wet, or color the water red when an infested cat is bathed. On a dark surface, you may also notice what look like grains of salt; these are flea eggs. The larval stage, which look like miniscule worms, are rarely noticed.

Control must be exercised both on the cats themselves and on the environment. Whichever methods you use, remember to follow directions closely, not to use two products in conjunction, and not to use any product too often: what can kill a flea can also kill a cat in a large enough dosage. Be particularly careful in maternity wards, with young kittens, or around ailing cats.

Design your cattery for effective flea control. In part, of course, this means ease of cleaning, but there is yet another means of controlling fleas through physical design. Most fleas cannot jump more than twelve inches off the ground. By building your cattery floors higher than this, you will prevent fleas coming in from surrounding areas (this is especially a problem with outdoor cages) and from jumping onto your cat. Better yet, build cage floors from wood slats or some material that will allow fleas and flea eggs to drop through to the floor beneath. (Be sure any gaps in the floor are very narrow so paws and pads cannot be pinched). The floor underneath the cages can be regularly sprayed or powdered with insecticide to kill the fleas that have fallen through. Liquid and other debris will also fall through, helping to keep the cages above dry and clean.

If your cats have the freedom of the house, frequent vacuuming is a must. Put some flea powder into the vacuum bag to kill fleas that are caught or hatch inside the bag. An insecticidal spray can be sprayed into crevices and any other places you cannot reach with the vaccum. Be sure to distinguish between sprays that can be used directly on the cat and general-purpose sprays, which are more powerful and should never be sprayed directly on the cat. If you use a steam carpet cleaner, put a little flea dip into the water used. A little flea dip can also be used in the rinse cycle when washing cat bedding.

Flea bombs emit a fog which reaches all the nooks and crannies; read directions carefully (all living things, including house plants, must be removed before you fog). One or two repetitions of the fogging procedure should be made to hit the newly-hatched fleas, since the fog will not kill the flea eggs; space the foggings two to three weeks apart. New fogs on the market are dual-action; that is, they kill both the adult fleas and leave a residual film that kills hatching larvae.

On the cats themselves, you have a choice of sprays, powders, shampoos, dips, and collars.

Flea shampoos kill the fleas on the cat but have little residual effect. Note that ordinary shampoos will *not* kill fleas: the flea will get wet and inactive and may appear dead, but once the cat's fur begins to dry the flea revives. You end up with just as many fleas – cleaner fleas. Flea powders are cheap and efficient, but the powder seldom remains in the fur more than a day or so. Flea dips can be used on a dry cat *or* a wet cat after bathing; they have a residual effect of five to ten days and are very effective but should not be used too often. The sprays are similar, though many breeders dislike them because the cat inevitably breathes in a great deal of spray, whereas with the powder or dip the face can be protected.

Flea collars and medallions last three to five months, but are not much in use by breeders – in fact, I've never heard of any breeder using them. There are several problems with them. Many cats develop allergies to the collars resulting in sores and hair loss on the neck. A medallion can dip into the water as the cat drinks, causing contamination. If your cats are social groomers, they may also lick a flea collar or medallion on another cat.

Brewer's yeast is recommended by some: a teaspoon daily per cat seems to create a body odor fleas don't like. If you try this technique, you'd better dose yourself too, lest the fleas find you tasty. There are other products the cat ingests orally that are supposed to control fleas by entering the cat's bloodstream, so that when the flea takes a meal it's his last. I've never tried these products, as the topical (surface) products seem much safer and quite effective.

Almost every species of land mammal has a corresponding species of flea. In general, dog fleas will stay on dogs and cats fleas on cats, although if a flea cannot locate the correct host he'll opt for a second choice. Cat owners are seldom bitten by cat fleas, even in a flea-infested household. There *is* a species of human flea, now very rare. It's quite large, sluggish and doesn't jump (which tells us something about cat vs. human abilities at flea catching). The human fleas were used in Victorian flea circuses. A few flea circuses still exist in England, and the story goes that a certain man in Manchester allows himself to be a flea habitat in order to replenish the supply of human fleas. Cat and dog fleas are much too agile to be used in a flea circus.

Adapting your home to cats

Cats and kittens are destructive only *en masse,* and it would take at least two dozen to equal the capacity for chaos inherent in one puppy – or child.

However, cat breeding and fine furniture do not go together well. Even those breeders with deluxe caging in buildings separate from their homes usually have several cats wadering through the house — after all, if they didn't love cats enough to want them around you, why would they be interested in breeding?

One or two cats can be trained not to sharpen their claws on the Louis Quinze sofa, but anyone with more than a few cats soon gives up hope and resigns himself to tattered furniture. So if you have fine furniture, sell it, put in into a non-cat room, or cover it with padding. Or buy leather and vinyl: these are safe from being used as scratching posts, as are some very tight weaves of cloth. Some cat breeders have living rooms that look like they came from St Vincent de Paul's, and if the breeders are smart, they probably did.

Wooden furniture will acquire surface scratches from cats jumping on and off. When this happens, recall those stores that beat new furniture with chains to "antique" it quickly, or the Persian carpets put out on the sidewalk to become worn and doubly valuable, and be grateful to your cats for doing the job for you.

There is not a kitten alive that has not swung from the drapes or thrown up on the carpet, so if your non-living possessions are more precious to you than the living and breathing — don't breed cats.

Other adaptations you must make will include keeping such items as rubber bands, string, thread, paper clips and so forth well out of reach of cats and kittens. If kittens are free in the house, you must keep toilets closed or eventually one will fall in and drown. You must be careful lest kittens crawl into cupboards, closets, washers, dryers, and refrigerators. Doors must be shut with caution to avoid catching tails, and rocking chairs should be disposed of entirely, as well as recliners with mechanisms that could trap a paw or tail. Carpeting can be such a problem, especially in effective flea control, that you should dispense with it altogether if possible, or buy a high-powered cleaner.

Everyone who has raised kittens underfoot has had to learn what I call the "kitten shuffle," for fear of stepping on a baby that hasn't learned or isn't quick enough to get out of the way.

Dogs in the household may not be a problem at all; some take a motherly attitude to young kittens. Children may not be as respectful of new life, and should be taught to handle the kittens properly, not to attempt to play with them before they are old enough, or experiment with them to see what happens when, for instance, they are put into the dishwasher.

Food and feeding

Unlike humans, most cats actually prefer a monotonous diet. Once you've found a feeding plan that suits both you and your cats, stick to it. Constantly changing because other breeders or articles say your cats can't simply *cannot* be healthy without the addition of *x* will put your cats under stress and play havoc with their digestive systems.

Most breeders allow their cats access throughout the day to a bowl of kibble (dry food). Prepared meals are fed once or twice a day with an extra meal or two for weanling kittens or pregnant and lactating queens. These consist of raw meat, cooked meat, canned food or a combination of these, plus a vitamin supplement. Fresh, clean water must be always available. The variations on this basic plan are endless.

Concerning vitamins: there are many brands especially formulated for cats. These come in tablet form, powders, or liquids. The powders are probably best because you can mix them into the food and they are highly palatable, whereas not all cats will eat the tablets. The liquid vitamins are useful for weanling kittens.

Avoid adding one or two vitamins arbitrarily, thinking perhaps that a pregnant queen needs more of one thing or another. You may put the entire diet out of kilter and cause unnecessary problems.

Milk is not digestible by many cats after weaning and can cause diarrhea. Evaporated milk or KMR (or the kitten formula given later) is better tolerated and can be fed during the last two weeks of pregnancy and during lactation; however, except for weanling kittens, milk and milk-based formulae should *not* be considered dietary staples.

Whether or not all fresh meats should be cooked is a disputed question; most breeders would agree that pork and fish should always be cooked, while chicken, beef and organ meats can be fed raw.

Specially formulated diets are available in canned, semi-moist and dry foods from veterinarians, pet shops and other outlets (not at the supermarkets). These are more expensive than the standard commercial foods but tend to be a higher quality with less water weight, and so may actually be more economical in the long run.

Commercial canned and dry foods supplemented with a few tidbits will be quite adequate for most cats and are used by many, many breeders, though they might not feel inclined to boast about it. Normally only large breeders concoct the elaborate diets that take hours to prepare. If you buy a kitten from such a breeder, listen respectfully to her advice but don't feel obligated to follow it. Ask your veterinarian what he recommends when you take your kitten in for its post-purchase examination.

Look for products labelled "nutritionally complete" and give those preference. The generic foods are almost never adequate nutrition for cats, and the few dollars you save by purchasing them may result in many dollars spent later on vet bills. It shouldn't be necessary to add that commercial dog food should not be fed to cats.

Most problem eaters are those cats that live alone; cats in company will be encouraged to eat. Overweight and underweight are both common problems with breeding animals. Overweight is easy to control; the underweight cat can be a problem, however.

Besides palatibility of food, consider cats' preferences as to *how* food is served. First, feed all canned and raw foods on saucers or shallow bowls. Cats, especially the short-nosed breeds, don't like to put their heads down into a deep feeding dish. Don't used plastic except for dry food; it absorbs odors and more finicky cats will find this distasteful. Separate all food into small pea-sized bits. Food stored in the refrigerator should have the chill taken off in a microwave, by standing out, or by the addition of boiling water. Never feed a spoonful of sticky glop straight from the refrigerator — you wouldn't want to eat it either.

Foods to try in addition to the basic diet: cottage cheese, yogurt, eggs (but not raw whites), baby cereal. Some cats love tomato juice and green leafy vegetables. Others like popcorn, chocolate bars, and oatmeal. Malt extract (a good hairball remedy) is a favorite treat, and very concentrated calories.

Safety in the cattery

Every person with cats should consider the possibility of fire in the home or cattery. This is particularly true of breeders who keep many caged cats, but even a sheltered house cat may not know enough to leave the house which has been her only refuge for the outdoors of which she is almost unaware, even if the way out is clear.

Smoke detectors should be kept in every part of the house and cattery. Carriers can be arranged near the cats' quarters for quick evacuation. A sign by all entrances stating that there are live animals inside — and where they are kept — can save your cats' lives if you aren't at home. For those with many cats I would even suggest a trial run to see how quickly and efficiently cats can be evacuated. A neighbor could be entrusted with a key for emergencies when you are absent.

You cannot train a cat not to play with electrical cords, but you *can* furnish more interesting playthings. Use the same care with cats that you would use with children. Keep breakables, medicines and cleaning solutions tightly sealed and out of reach. Pick up rubber bands, string, paper clips, nails, and other small objects promptly before they can be swallowed.

Other hazards include appliances the cat can crawl into such as the refrigerator, dryers, and ovens; objects in which cats can be trapped such as plastic bags, open furnace outlets, full bathtubs, open toilets.

Cats and house plants don't go well together: you may return home one day to find your plants denuded and your cats ill. If you must have plants, try growing a container of grass (genuine grass, that is) to entice the cats; they may then leave other plants alone.

The list of household products dangerous to cats if ingested or contacted is long and continually changing as new products come on the market. The best routine is to keep *all* cleaning compounds away from the cats and to use only those determined safe for cats in crowded cattery rooms or maternity quarters. Your vet can advise you on these products, or you can find them listed in veterinary and pet supply catalogs or in pet shops.

Catching escapees

If you discover that a cat has escaped the confines of the house or cattery, avoid excitement: noise and frenzied searching can drive the cat further away. Go out with a favorite toy, sit in one spot, and call the cat softly. Leave open the door or window from which the cat escaped — having secured the other cats, of course — and the cat may make its way back inside. Take a quiet friend of the escapee outside and sit with it; the other may feel more confident when it sees its friend and be drawn out of hiding. If the cat is not frightened but merely having a stroll, it shouldn't be hard to catch; only cats that are used to being chased will know enough to run away.

If an immediate search fails to turn up the escapee, try alerting neighborhood children and offering a reward, advertising in newspapers, posting signs on community bulletin boards. Contact the local animal shelters every day. Homebody cats that know and trust you shouldn't be too hard to catch. But what a nightmare if a visiting queen or newcomer escapes! Such cats should be doubly secured.

The cattery calendar and scheduling

Use a monthly calendar to note down such things as when annual shots are due for each cat. Try to get all your adult cats on the same schedule so that you won't be bothered with vaccinations staggered through the year. A cat that has had its vaccinations in the summer will not be harmed by having them again six months later to get it on schedule with the other cats. A good time of year to arrange an *en masse* vaccination program is during the off-breeding season from about November to January; this way you can avoid the possible spread of infection to pregnant queens.

Dates of mating should be carefully noted; if you don't write these down *at once* they're easy to forget. It's of utmost importance to know when the kittens are due. If the mating has taken place over two or three days, as is common, write down the first day that a breeding was witnessed. Also write onto the calendar, if no record is kept elsewhere, the stud to which your queen was mated if you have more than one stud or if you sent her to an outside stud service. Large breeders with several studs may not remember later which was used for your queen; not everyone keeps good records.

Counting from the date of breeding for each queen, indicate on the calendar for each one the twenty-first day (the day on which "pinking up" of the nipples can usually be noted if the queen has conceived), the fifty-eighth day after mating (the earliest day on which the birth of live kittens can be expected), and the sixty-third day (kittening normally falls between the sixty-third and sixty-fifth days after mating).

As soon as the kittens are born, write this too up on the calendar along with the number of days gestation. You don't want to be in doubt about the date of birth when you get ready to fill out the registration forms. Knowing the number of days gestation can be helpful when the queen kittens again, as most queens gestate exactly the same number of days for each litter (after the first, which tends to be early).

Shows and closing dates for entries can also be noted on the calendar along with which cat has been entered (yes, people *do* show up with the wrong cat), and special tasks such as worming (a quarterly or twice-yearly task), major flea-control operations, veterinary appointments, and so forth.

The well-stocked cattery

Vaccines for panleukopenia (distemper) and rhino/calici virus should be stored in the refrigerator unless otherwise noted. Heat can destroy the vaccines; they are always shipped airmail in special insulated containers. Keep vaccines tightly wrapped. Properly stored, vaccines should retain their effectiveness for about a year. When preparing to vaccinate cats or kittens, remove from the refrigerator only the vaccines needed (in the syringe, if using a multi-dose vial) and allow them to come to room temperature before injection.

Disposable plastic syringes and needles are included in the cost of the vaccine or purchased separately. These are so inexpensive, safe, and easy to use that it makes little sense to purchase the reusable sort. Each comes in a sealed plastic container that should be opened only immediately before use to maintain sterility. If you use these, store and dispose of them with the utmost caution, especially if you have children.

Mild opthalmic ointment for minor eye irritations, common in cats and young kittens, is useful to have on hand.

Keep a bulb thermometer for taking rectal temperature. Normal temperature range is from 101 to 102.5 degrees. Be sure to use only a thermometer made for cats. Lubricate the thermometer with a little petroleum jelly and insert gently into the rectum about half an inch. You may have to wait a moment for the sphincter muscle to relax before you can slide the thermometer in. Wait two minutes before withdrawing, and clean the thermometer well after each use.

Cold sterilizer is handy for sterilizing thermometers, hemostats, aspirators, feeding tubes, syringes, metal combs and other breeding and grooming apparatus. A small amount mixed with water in a bowl will last for two or three weeks.

It's a good idea to trim claws regularly, and you *must* trim them before showing. There are special clippers made for cats, but I've found that the small pincer-type clippers commonly sold for human use work adequately.

Worming tablets are best purchased from your veterinarian; the commercial types may not be effective for local conditions.

Fulvicin is a series-type tablet used to control ringworm; this too can be purchased from your vet. Most vets are not accustomed to working with cat breeders and may not think to ask if you have a pregnant queen, so be sure that *you* ask about the safety of any drug or vaccine you may purchase from your vet; fulvicin is one drug that must never be used during pregnancy.

Flea-control products such as specially-formulated shampoos, powders, sprays, flea-bombs, and so on.

Shampoos for regular bathing before a show; these can also be used after a flea shampoo, which tends to leave the coat a bit sticky. There are special shampoos formulated for cats; dog shampoos, baby shampoos and very mild detergents also work well.

Grass can be grown in a window-box for the cats to nibble on daily; many cats seem to need grass as a tonic or aid in digestion. Eating grass, if the cat is unaccustomed to doing so, can occasionally cause vomiting.

Malt extract preparation for hairballs; this is especially enjoyed by cats and can be given weekly (or daily in very small amounts) on the tip of a finger for the cat to lick off.

Food, food dishes and vitamin supplements; see the section on feeding for recommendations.

Treat your cats to an occasional "trip" on catnip. The reaction to catnip is fascinating; some queens present their vulvas and tread with their hind legs as though they were in heat. Prepubescent cats normally show little interest in catnip. Regular toys can include paper sacks, large cardboard tubes, and ping-pong balls. Use care in selecting toys; even those specially made for cats have been found to contain toxic ingredients.

Grooming combs; the Belgian combs or their imitators are the accepted ones. These are metal combs with long, wide teeth. Narrow-tooth combs such as flea combs can tear out the coat and shouldn't be used on a show cat. On shorthairs and non-show cats, a baby brush can be a real delight for the cat. For removing mats, nothing works better than a seam-ripper, sold in all sewing ships. In dry winter weather, static electricity can be controlled by rubbing the cat lightly with a de-static towel such as those sold for laundry use. Grooming powder and dry shampoos can brighten and fluff the coat between shampoos. For routine cleaning of ears, powdered boric acid on a cotton swab, used gently of couse, works well and cats don't object to it as they do to any form of liquid. Used twice daily for two or three weeks, boric acid can sometimes eliminate those persistent little ear mites.

Litter, litter boxes, baking soda or specially-formulated sprays for odor control, for the cats' sanitary needs. Small pans that can be changed daily are a better idea than one or two big, deep pans. Have twice as many as you will use at any one time, so that half can be soaking in a cleaning solution while the other half are in use.

Special cleaning compounds and disinfectants for catteries. Almost any cleaning compound can be used safely in your house, as long as the cat doesn't come in contact with it before it dries or have a chance to ingest it. Where cats are confined, however, use those you *know* are safe.

First aid for cats

The first step in aiding a stricken cat is to catch and confine it. Injured cats should be handled carefully and gently with their welfare and yours in mind. A badly frightened and injured cat is likely to strike out at anything and everything. If this seems likely, throw a large towel or bedspread over the cat and wrap it gently but securely, or you can drop a box over the cat and slide the lid underneath. If the cat is unconcious, lift it carefully, supporting head, shoulders and pelvis, and place it on a flat carrier such as a piece of board.

Before calling or rushing off to the vet, take a moment to examine the cat. Note whether the cat is limping or dragging a leg. Note the breathing and the color of the gums. Looks for wounds and signs of bleeding, and apply a tourniquet if needed. If poisoning is a possibility, determine what type of substance was ingested. Tube-feeding equipment can be used to extract liquid poisons from the stomach or to dilute the stomach contents. Semi-solid or powdered poisons can be partially flushed out by forcing water into the stomach and then withdrawing it repeatedly. Call your veterinarian if you're not sure about attempting these procedures, and be sure to have him check your cat afterwards, even if your treatment proved effective.

Since catteries strictly control their cats' housing, the major cause of cat injuries — the automobile — can be discounted. If there are loose dogs or dog packs in your neighborhood, make doubly sure that the cats cannot get out, since many home-raised cats will not know how or where to escape from dog attacks.

Cattery or home accidents, when they do occur, usually involve falls resulting in broken bones, especially among kittens, but these are seldom serious unless the spine is fractured. Kittens *must* be allowed freedom to run, jump, and climb, and it's cruel to cage young kittens in an attempt to prevent injuries. I recall from my riding days a magnificent Arabian stallion kept in a stall at a boarding stable. I never once saw him out of his stall; he wasn't used for riding. Wouldn't it be kinder, as well as cheaper, I asked, to keep him at pasture? I was told that the horse was much too valuable to ever let loose in a pasture, where there was a chance that he might injure himself. I'm sure he lived out his days in that padded stall. This is nonsense, of course. The most valuable of all stallions, the top Thoroughbred sires, have paddocks and pastures in which to exercise, and the possibility of injury is really quite small. But there *are* breeders who raise their kittens in small cages up till the day they are sold for exactly the same reason.

Cat fights — not the occasional spat but real free-for-alls — will rarely if ever be a problem if your cats are allowed adequate space and freedom. If a fight should occur, don't jump into the middle of it. A good dousing with water or a counterattack with a handy broom are good ways of breaking it up. Such quarrels are most likely to be started by belligerent mothers whose babies are just starting to leave the nest.

Cat hierarchies

The cat is not a pack or herd animal and does not form strict hierarchies (pecking orders) as do dogs, cows and chickens. Cats kept together in small groups will live quite amicably together. One cat, usually an older, agressive queen, will sometimes emerge as the cat to which the others must defer, and an especially meek queen may bottom out as a scapegoat to the others. Tomcats form special heirarches of their own; mounting behavior by the dominant tom of the other toms is common. Neutered cats and kittens generally have no place in cat social hierarchies. New cats will be carefully investigated by all and put in their place by the dominant queen. Queens and toms alike, with the possible exception of the dominant queen, will take part in social grooming.

These heirarchies are not always strictly observed, and places can be temporarily reversed, especially when the cats are allowed a lot of space and freedom. The more crowded the conditions, the more rigid the social structure becomes. Confrontations and minor spats are common and you should not attempt to interfere by punishing one cat or comforting another.

Queens with litters of kittens rise immediately to the top of the social heap, whatever their placement has been previously. Some are so touchy that the slightest unaccustomed noise will provoke an immediate attack against the nearest cat, to the great surprise of the innocent one; even the dominant queen will flee from an irate mother. Some nursing queens seem to be looking for an excuse to wallop something. Humans are normally exempt, but be observant if strangers handle the young kittens. Oddly enough, the queen's protective instinct seem dormant as long as the kittens remain in the nest, and strongest when the kittens start to toddle around. I've seen a queen readily accept an intruder who decided to share the nest with her and her kittens, only to pounce on him once the kittens were older and had left the nest.

Feline Leukemia Virus

This book is not meant to replace a good health-care manual; however, the most common diseases and those which cat breeders actively test for will be reviewed.

Feline Leukemia Virus (FeLV) has been much in the news because of its similarities to the human AIDS virus, and because a vaccine for it has been successfully developed. The virus affects one out of fifty cats. After contracting this contagious disease a cat will either develop immunity or it will develop disease symptoms of variable types, including cancer, anemia, pneumonia, reproductive failure and other problems.

Its importance for the cat breeder lies in the fact that a cat that has developed immunity can be a carrier and infect other cats; therefore the presence of a FeLV carrier in the cattery should not be permitted.

A simple test will indicate which cats are positive for the virus and which are negative. The FeLV-positive cat is endangering all other cats and kittens in the cattery. The virus is thought to be transmitted through the saliva.

You should certainly make your pet buyers aware of the vaccine. Whether or not to vaccinate all your own cats is another matter. Your veterinarian may feel that you are better off without it. It is still quite new and less effective than other types of vaccines, and there have been some side effects. Certainly its value is immense to the cat whose environment is not controlled, but its value to the breeder is still somewhat in doubt.

Feline Infectious Peritonitis

FIP virus infection is widespread in cats, with approximately 25% of all cats having been infected. The percentage is higher in catteries and multi-cat households; almost all cats will have serum antibodies to the FIP virus. Titers can range from 1:25 to 1:400 and more. Some of these cats will be entirely immune to the disease, while others will be chronic carriers and can infect other cats and kittens. It is thought that cats with high antibody titers that remain high (discovered through a series of tests) are more likely to be carriers than those with low titers.

The primary infection with FIP can be so mild that it is not recognized by the breeder. Some cats will recover completely; others will develop related problems over weeks or months. Only a few FIP-virus infected cats develop the fatal form of the disease; this occurs primarily in younger cats and particularly very young kittens; hence the special importance of control for the breeder. The likelihood of kitten mortalities from FIP in a cattery is thought to relate to the proportion of older cats that have high antibody titers (1:400 or above).

Many breeders have their cats tested for FIP titers, and many fine breeding animals have been euthanized when found to have high titers. The test, however, does *not* reveal which cats are carriers and which are not. The major use of the FIP test, therefore, should be in diagnosis of the disease. Nevertheless, a few breeders will not buy a kitten or accept a queen for breeding unless they have been FIP-tested.

If you decide to do so, be aware that the interpretation of the test is variable and do not allow destruction of a cat with a high titer unless you are convinced that it poses a serious health threat to the other cats and kittens. Until the test results are more conclusive, many breeders and veterinarians alike will see no reason to use the test except on those cats suspected of having contracted the chronic form of the disease.

Too many breeders, with the worthwhile goal of maintaining health in their cattery, submit their animals to each and every new form of test as it becomes available.

Feline respiratory disease

Respiratory disease is second only to feline distemper (panleukopenia) as the most serious disease among cats. The term encompasses several diseases, but all are characterized by sneezing, tearing, inflammation of the eyes and nose, and discharge from the eyes and nose.

Rhinotracheitis is a highly contagious disease responsible for thirty to forty percent of all respiratory infections. It is the most serious of the respiratory diseases. Adults usually recover in seven to fourteen days; the death rate among kittens, however, is about fifty percent. Vaccines include an injectible vaccine and ocular-nasal drops; the former is now more widely used. Both stimulate production of antibodies which circulate in the bloodstream, and both require two doses to establish protection in the kitten. Annual revaccination (one dose) is advised thereafter.

Calicivirus infection is also widespread; it infects both the respiratory tract and the mouth, causing tongue ulcers which may make the cat refuse to eat. Death rate is low, but higher among kittens. The vaccine for calicivirus is combined with the rhinotracheitis vaccine.

Feline pneumonitis is the mildest of the three diseases; it is caused by the Chlamydia virus. The symptoms include a slight rise in temperature, watering from the eyes and a slight nasal discharge. Pneumonitis can be treated after infection has developed, whereas rhinotracheitis and calicivirus do not respond to antibiotics. Immunization against pneumonitis is sometimes also included in the rhino-calici vaccine, or it can be given separately.

Vaccination will protect the cat from many, but not all, respiratory diseases. There are other agents causing respiratory infection from which there is little protection other than maintaining a clean, stress-free environment and using care in introducing new cats.

Coccidiosis

The coccidia is a one-celled animal that lives in the small intestine, where it reproduces. The eggs are passed in the feces, where they must remain at least two days before they become infective. Symptoms of infection are bloody diarrhea, weight loss, dehydration and anemia. Treatment wil usually include sulfa drugs or antibiotics.

Coccidiosis is usually harmless to adult cats but can be a killer of newborn kittens. An aid to prevention is strict sanitation, in particular the changing of soiled litter daily before the infective stage of the eggs can be reached.

Routine worming

All cats and kittens, especially those fed a raw-meat diet, should be routinely wormed two to four times a year. Roundworms are a mild but persistent problem in many catteries. Safe and effective medication can be purchased from your vet or a vet-supply house. If your cats begin to vomit, lose condition and develop a coarse coat texture, worms might be the problem.

Many catteries also worm regularly for tapeworms. Tapeworms are carried by cat fleas, so if you have a flea problem you will almost certainly have a tapeworm problem too. Tapeworms are only debilitating in very young or sick cats, or if infestation is extremely heavy. Nevertheless, they must be controlled. The worm segments are passed from the anus; when live, they can be seen to stretch and move. When dried, they resemble sesame seeds. Your vet can prescribe worming tablets.

A warning against medicating cats yourself

Some cat breeders, upon discovering the ease with which they can perform simple procedures such as vaccinations and wormings, decide that veterinarians are superfluous and begin medicating their cats themselves. This attitude is both dangerous and irresponsible. Breeders who wish to become expert in veterinary medicine should apply to a veterinary college. Breeders must also be aware of *fads* in medications and procedures that seem to migrate regularly through clubs and breeders' circles. New products should be discussed with a vet before use. Too many fine cats have been cripped or killed due to their owner's mismanagement.

However, every cat owner and breeder *can* learn how to examine their cats regularly, how to interpret various signs, and how to exercise preventive health measures.

Chapter Four: *Breeding Theory*

The meaning of purebred

A cat is considered a purebred if it is a member of a recognized breed or has five generations of like-to-like breeding behind it. A breed may have one primary characteristic with which it is associated – for example, the folded ears of the Scottish Fold – but the breed standard will specify all areas of coat, color and conformation, and a purebred will approach this standard in all areas.

There was little concern in the past for pure blood or the mating of like to like. Our practical forefathers were concerned with results, not some tenuous attribute called "purity." And the record has shown that purity is by no means the *ne plus ultra* the layman believes it to be. For example, when the Arabian horse was crossed with horses distinctly *unlike* itself – cold-blooded English mares – the resulting progeny, the Thoroughbred, far surpassed the centuries-old Arabian in size, speed, and athletic ability.

Even today, Irish draft horses are bred to Thoroughbred stallions to produce the finest hunters in the world, and Germany's Hanoverian registry, source of multiple Olympic winners, approves individual horses of various other breeds for its own breeding program.

Such practices go against the grain of most animal breeders, whose mania for "blood purity" echoes the Third Reich. Yet a breed, like a strain within a breed, will at some point reach the limit of its potential and necessitate an infusion of outside blood.

Why, then, should we limit ourselves to the resources of one breed's genetic pool? Instead of spending our time searching for bend sinisters in pedigrees, let's be concerned with results, for that is what breeding should be about: a matter of *predictable results*. Take two queens that look exactly alike, one a purebred and one a domestic, and breed them to a purebred tom, and you'll see the value of predictable results. But do not accord an equal status to every cat called "purebred," for genetic purity, like multi-generation pedigrees, means little in and of itself. It is important only in terms of the individual breeding animal or program to which it applies.

Just as an alleycat can have a pedigree, an ugly, nasty-tempered and sickly cat can be a purebred, though I hope nobody would want to perpetuate such an animal.

Basic Color & Pattern Inheritance

I. Black and its Dilution, Blue

(The color in parentheses means that the cat carries this color recessively, i.e., unseen. The presence of recessives can be determined from the pedigree or from test matings.)

(1) Black x Black	All Black
(2) Black (blue) x Black	All Black
(3) Black (blue) x Black (blue)	3 Black : 1 Blue
(4) Black x Blue	All Black
(5) Black (blue) x Blue	1 Black : 1 Blue
(6) Blue x Blue	All Blue

The proportions also apply to:

Coat Length: substitute Shorthair for black and Longhair for blue
Chocolate: substitute Chocolate for black and Lilac for blue
Colorpoints: substitute Non-Colopoint for black and Colorpoint for blue
Rex Coat: substitute Non-Rex for black and Rex for blue
White (masking): substitute White for black and non-white for blue
White (spotting): substitute Spotted for black and Non-Spotted for blue
Tabby: substitute Tabby for black and Non-Tabby (Solid) for blue
Silver: substitute Silver for black and Non-Silver for blue

II. Orange and Tortoiseshell

(Sex-linked colors)

(1) Orange male x Non-Orange female	Non-Orange male : Tortie female
(2) Non-Orange male x Orange female	Orange male : Tortie female
(3) Orange male x Tortie female	Non-Orange male : Orange male : Orange female : Tortie female
(4) Non-Orange male x Tortie female	Non-Orange male : Orange male : Non-Orange female : Tortie female

The "Non-Orange" color can be black, blue, chocolate, or lilac, and can be combined with various patterns, i.e., tortie-and-white equals calico.
Cream and blue-cream are, respectively, the dilutions of Orange and Tortie.

For a complete look at this very complex subject, see *Genetics for Cat Breeders* by Roy Robinson, Pergamon Press, 1977, or *Cat Genetics* by A C Jude, TFH Publications, 1967.

Terminology: genetics

An animal has both a *phenotype,* or outward appearance, and a *genotype,* or genetic make-up. Part of the genotype can be determined from the outward appearance. For example, if a *dominant* gene is present, such as the gene for a short coat or the color black, it will be visible. Part of the genotype can be hidden. A black shorthair cat can carry genes for longhair and for the color blue, both *recessive* traits. A longhaired blue cat — both recessives — must be *homozygous* for these two traits: one gene for color and coat length was received from each parent, and in this case, both genes are the same. A shorthair black cat can also be homozygous for black and for shorthair, if it received identical genes from both parents for these features. However, it may also be *heterozygous* if it carries long coat and blue as hidden recessives, and these can be passed to its offspring. An animal is homozygous or heterozygous only in respect to a gene pair; the whole animal is homozygous for some features and heterozygous for others. An animal that is homozygous for a large percentage of genes will be *prepotent,* since the variation in genes it passes to the next generation will be smaller than in the largely heterozygous animal.

When cats are bred together, they can be *inbred* or *outcrossed.* Inbreeding is the mating of near relatives; outcrossing is the mating of unrelated individuals. The term *linebreeding* is also used for less intense inbreeding.

Genetics and breeding practice

Genetics is a science still in its infancy. For all the claims made by the press, you'd think the work of the breeder an anachronism. Mechanical manipulation of genetic material is, we're told, just around the corner. According to such reports, the scientist has only to prod a chromosome in order to produce a best-in-show winner in a matter of seconds rather than years. But I suspect there's a little more to it than that.

Books and articles on animal genetics concern themselves mainly with color genetics, leaving to the realm of shadows all the other characteristics that make up the living animal. Perhaps this is because the colors and patterns are so highly visible and because they tend to follow the "rules." The color genetics of cats are of particular interest to geneticists because of the large variety of colors and patterns and the sex-linked color. The chart at the beginning of this chapter shows basic color inheritance.

Prepotency

A breed is created when its characteristics are *fixed* by breeding to other animals with the same characteristics. In most breeds, and in cats particularly, this has been done by breeding together closely-related animals. In many cases every cat in the breed can be traced back to a very small group of ancestors. The continual breeding together of inter-related cats results in the *fixing* of breed characteristics by raising the level of homozygosity in the breed population.

Every purebred animal is prepotent to a certain degree: and herein lies the value of breeds. A high degree of homozygosity can result in a breed that is extremely *prepotent,* that is, likely to pass on its characteristics to its progeny, even when bred to an unrelated animal.

The best explanation for prepotency is that such individuals have a very high degree of homozygosity and therefore are more likely than not to be inbred. In a brother-to-sister mating, for example, we can expect that 25% of the gene pairs will be made homozygous; in a father-to-daughter mating, 12.5% (actual percentages will vary; these are probabilities only). The figure increases if ancestors are also inbred. It is possible, though much more unlikely, for two unrelated individuals to produce a prepotent animal.

Among purebred animals, only the Arabian horse, product of centuries of close breeding, is renowned for the prepotency of the entire breed. But in *every* species and breed, prepotent individuals exist that stamp all their progeny with their likeness. Again among horses, such an animal was Justin Morgan, an individual so prepotent that an entire breed was created from him, though his ancestry was unknown (what with the fanaticism about purebreds and registration, Justin Morgan wouldn't have a chance today).

Individuals, breeds, and strains within breeds can be more or less prepotent than others. As a breeder, you should attempt to determine the prepotency of your breeding animals, especially the sires, by *progeny testing,* and in your study of other strains and animals in your breed, you should keep a sharp eye out for any exceptionally prepotent cats.

Most breeds have a few studs that stand out as especially prepotent (a queen can be equally prepotent, but her lifetime production is much smaller than the tom's and therefore carries less import).

Keep in mind that an animal can be prepotent for *poor* characteristics as well as good. Prepotency is valuable only in terms of the individual. A purebred cat of impeccable ancestry is no more valuable to a breeding program than the alleycat nextdoor, unless it is able to pass on its high merit to succeeding generations.

Progeny Testing

If you're breeding with the primary goal of producing show cats, you will have to *progeny test* every cat. A sample of four litters — about twelve to sixteen kittens — will serve as an accurate indicator of a queen's genetic makeup. If no excellent kittens are produced, the queen should be replaced, whether this means finding a new home for her or altering her to keep as a pet. Of course, the male's influence shouldn't be overlooked; perhaps the two cats simply didn't "click" together. Switching to another male after one or two unsatisfactory litters might be wise. Progeny testing of males should proceed along the same lines, and will generally take less time since he can produce many more kittens than a single queen.

If your cats are from top-producing bloodlines, or are truly superb individuals, progeny testing can extend into the second generation, particularly in the case of an outcross. When a breeding-quality queen is outcrossed to a top-show tom, for example, a male and female kitten could be kept and bred together, or a female kitten could be bred back to her sire. Long-range planning of this type will prevent you from discarding prematurely those cats whose true breeding worth doesn't reveal itself until the second generation.

Inbreeding and outcrossing

Most human societies have been prejudiced against inbreeding, and this prejudice is often carried into animal breeding. The term *linebreeding* was coined to bypass this bias, though the distinction between the two is nebulous. It seems that whenever a queen miscarries or a male proves infertile or kittens die *in utero,* the breeder will say "I guess I was breeding too close." Unless, of course, the mating was an outcross, in which case diet, weather, or the phase or the moon will be blamed.

Inbreeding will increase prepotency, result in kittens that have a similar look, i.e., a true strain, and can be used to fix the characteristics of an outstanding individual for future generations. The main problem with inbreeding is that unwanted recessives will come to light. *All* humans and animals carry genes that can cause deformities, early death, poor development, etc. These genes survive because they are recessive. If they were dominant, they'd result in death, poor fertility, or inability to catch prey, and thus would not be passed on to the next generation. There are certain exceptions, such as genes that affect an animal only after its breeding life is over.

Inbreeding brings these unwanted recessives to light because both parents, being closely related, have probably inherited the same recessive genes. If an inbred animal is outcrossed, its unwanted recessives will remain hidden behind the dominant genes of the unrelated animal: the recessive must be passed on by both parents before it can be made visible. This can happen when the animal is bred to a sibling, parent, or cousin. This bringing to light of unwanted recessives is undesirable, of course, among humans: thus the ages-old prejudice against inbreeding. But the cat is a prolific enough breeder that the occasional appearance of an unwanted recessive will not be disastrous. Moreover, with each generation of inbreeding the strain is further purified as the recessives are weeded out.

Each generation of inbreeding will *fix* the characteristics of the foundation animals, until eventually a high degree of uniformity will be produced in all kittens. Cats that are outcrossed will vary much more: within each litter there may be one superb kitten, two mediocre kittens, and one or two dreadfuls (according to the breed standard). If the breeder only wants one or two superior kittens to show and is not concerned with creating a unique strain or raising the average merit of her kittens, outcrossing superior animals is a good route to success.

Inbred individuals are not always superior show animals, but they're generally preferred for breeding because they will produce offspring that fall within a narrow range of fixed characteristics, and because some of those characteristics are known in advance and can therefore be compensated for. Since perfect individuals are seldom produced, it makes sense to choose our breeding stock for its faults rather than its virtues. If, therefore, the line is known for excellent coats but tends to have poor eye color, we will prefer a cat with an average coat but excellent eye color to the one with superb coat but poor eye color, since the one breaks away from the general trend and is therefore more valuable. The first cat has a better chance of producing offspring with both good coats and eye color than does the second. Such selection will have to be balanced by the priority given each feature, based on the point scale of the breed standard.

Many breeders believe that outcrossing gives a better chance of producing an outstanding individual than does inbreeding. This has been borne out many times in practice. Outcrossing produces a much greater *range in quality* in the individuals produced. The characteristics of the parents, or of the parent's bloodlines, do not match. As an extreme example, take the breeding together of two very different dog breeds; say a Bulldog and a Golden Retriever. The pups produced will range from those resembling their sire to those resembling their dam and everything in between. Rarely, a pup may be produced that looks like a purebred of one of the breeds. The breeding together of two mongrel dogs, in which *no* characteristics have been fixed, results sometimes in an extraordinary variety of pups.

By outcrossing within a breed we will produce the occasional individual that is far superior to either parent or to any of its ancestors due to a fortunate combination of genes. But this animal is not necessarily a superior breeding animal.

Hybrid vigor

A hybrid is an animal that results from the crossing of two species, such as the mule (donkey x horse). Hybrids often have better health and endurance than either parent; they are usually sterile. The term hybrid can also be used to define the product of crossing two breeds or even two unrelated strains within a breed, though the more common term for the latter would be outcross.

Outcrossing results in a heterozygous animal in which hybrid vigor is to some degree usually apparent.

Kittens that are the result of outcrossing are thought to have a stronger grip on life than inbred kittens. Because of the great variability, a few excellent kittens may be born, as well as a few very poor ones. Many top show cats are the result of outcrosses.

However, the breeder mustn't ignore the long-term picture. What happens when the spectacular, outcrossed show cat is bred? All too often, a falling off in quality. The outcrossed cat's genotype is largely unknown, and he may be entirely lacking in the ability to transmit his excellent features to his offspring.

The Catch-22 of animal breeding

Breeders select for the extremes, but nature tends towards the mean.

Remember this rule if you're working with one of the extreme breeds, i.e. those with characteristics that deviate widely from the norm. If you breed a Persian with a correct short, snubbed nose and a Persian with a long straight nose, the kittens (in respect to noses) will range between the two, but will tend toward the *mean* of the species as a whole: the longer "alleycat" nose. If you breed together two cats that both have the correct extreme nose, more kittens will have a correct nose, but there will *still* be a tendency towards the mean of the species as a whole; again, you'll get some long, straight noses. Breed together two alleycats, however, and you'll almost never get that short snub nose: nature tends only towards the mean. Only inbreeding can fix extreme characteristics by creating animals that are homozygous for the desired trait. This can happen within a strain by inbreeding over several generations. It will happen in the breed as a whole over a much longer period of time.

Myths and mistakes

"Quality, not quantity" is a corollary to "I'm not in it for the money," both statements to which cat breeders are enamoured. But an animal is not a manufactured product where craftsmanship and economy are at odds. In animal breeding, because of the large part played by chance, quality and quantity go hand in hand. The more throws of the dice the better the chance of getting just the combination you want. Of course, the breeder must be sure to put fortune in her favor by following the general principles of good breeding and by guarding the health of her stock.

What about the slow-developing line? If you haven't heard this from a breeder yet, you're a raw novice. When a breeder claims that she has a "slow-developing" line, she means that if the show kitten you bought looks bad at twelve weeks or five months or eight months, just hang in there, give it some time and it's going to knock 'em dead in the show ring before too much longer. The cat may die of old age before reaching the degree of perfection some breeders promise.

Of course, breeds and bloodlines *do* have different stages of development, and sometimes tend to look ill-proportioned and awkward. A cat can indeed "come together" when it matures. It can just as easily fall apart, but few breeders mention this. If breeders know their bloodlines well enough to predict the changes that will be visible, they should tell their show-kitten customers what to look for, and when, and not merely that it is a slow-developing line.

Some experienced breeders seem to think they're the only persons in their breed who know what they're doing. Let a newcomer make a great success out of a few mediocre cats, and it's just luck. Let an old-timer finally make it to the top, and it's her just reward after years of hard work. But let the breeder with The System do well, and she at once assumes the air of a potentate.

In reality, every breeding plan is going to be restricted by the cats you are able to buy, the studs you can find to breed to, and which cats will consent to breed together. The best-made plans can be thwarted by a kitten death, a tom's infertility, a queen's inability to carry kittens to term, or, if nothing else, the failure of your cats to stick unerringly to the percentages.

Group perfection

"I'd have a perfect cat if only I could take the coat from one, the head from another, the color from another, and the eyes from yet another and combine them all into one cat."

Although cats don't lend themselves to this sort of piecing together, you can make use of the same idea in aiming for group perfection. Group perfection means that, although no one cat will be ideal in all aspects, the group of cats as a whole comprise perfection in every point, according to the breed standard. If you start with and maintain your breeding stock according to this rule, your cats may one day produce for you the kitten that has it all. Conversely, if you allow your breeding group to become deficient in one or more features, it's likely that all the kittens produced will also be deficient.

Few of us can start with Grand Champion-caliber cats, but we *can* start with a group that together could make up a Grand Champion, and one day will.

Give preference to the cat that is excellent in every respect except for one or two glaring faults, even if those faults disbar it from the show ring, over the cat with no faults that is mediocre in most characteristics. It is much easier to correct one or two faults by breeding than it is to raise the quality of the entire animal.

Copying other bloodlines

Should the beginning breeder attempt to duplicate the bloodlines of an established breeder? This sometimes happens when an enthusiast finds a mentor and purchases breeding stock only from that person. By doing so, she foregoes the chance to produce a line that is uniquely her own, and she may also lose the possibility of producing an outstanding cat early in her breeding program. After many generations a closely-bred strain can exhaust itself. The offspring fall within a continually narrowing range. With today's rapidly advancing breeds, a cat that's a winner in its youth may no longer be competitive in old age. Neither will its inbred kittens be competitive.

When a cat is a winner at the shows, or an obviously outstanding specimen, immediate inbreeding should follow its success in order to fix those characteristics. As the superior cats of the breed tend to progress beyond him, he should be less closely bred to (linebred), and finally, when he has become somewhat "old fashioned," outcrosses can be used to bring in new qualities while retaining some of the old.

Not all breeds are so volatile as to make this necessary. Some breeds of dogs are considered to have reached their peak of perfection at some point in the past, usually coinciding with a peak in popularity. The greater the population of a breed the greater the range: the finest as well as the poorest individuals are produced. In such a case, the breeder must try to maintain the highest point of perfection reached by closely inbreeding to the best individuals.

Creating your own strain

How long will it be before people begin to recognize cats from your cattery as belonging to your own unique strain? We are talking about two different things here: first, your cats all being members of a group with distinctly recognizable features (a homozygous population), and second, your cats being distinguishable from everyone else's in your breed, particularly the person from whom you purchased your foundation stock.

Surprisingly, a "new look" can make itself evident in the very first generation, especially if you are outcrossing into two different strains that just happen to click. To consolidate this look and make it universal to all your kittens will take two to three more generations.

If, however, you are breeding exclusively from an already established strain, your kittens will at first be recognizable as belonging to that strain and not a new one. But because people always select for slightly different qualities, you could still expect differences to become evident in about three generations, even if you never go outside your original stock.

Just because cat breeding has been in existence for a hundred years now, don't assume that it's taken that long to get where we are today in respect to the merits of individual breeds. If today's cats look better to us than those of thirty years ago, it's not necessarily because of progress. If Persian and Siamese breeders of thirty years ago had universally wanted to breed cats of our modern type — and if they had been able to visualize the look they wanted — we would have had our present-day show types much sooner. Often breeders don't know where they want to go until they're already there.

Unless *you* are able to visualize the ideal of your breed, you will never succeed in creating a strain. The best idea is to use an actual photograph of a cat you consider the most beautiful of its breed, and to bear that picture constantly in mind when selecting which cats to breed from. Otherwise you're likely to end up with a hodge-podge of, perhaps, some very fine cats, but nothing distinctively yours. The same thing will happen if you persist in buying new, completely unrelated cats at the drop of every rosette.

Progress in creating a strain depends largely on the number of kittens you have to select from, how close your foundation stock comes to your personal ideal, and on your breeding plan. The way to renown in the cat fancy — if renown is what you want — is to create a highly individual strain that consistently produces top show winners. Given patience, skill, lots of cats and a big measure of luck, you may one day find the world on your doorstep clamoring for kittens.

The small breeder, however, can only hope for modest gains unless she allies herself with other small breeders or a large breeder working towards the same goals. Still, success can come even to the small fry of the cat breeding world — and it's all the more to their credit, when it does.

Frequency of breeding the tom

With the entire male cat the problem is more likely to be too few queens than too many. Most toms are not used for outside stud work, and many are content with a small harem of three or four queens. A tom with no access to queens or too few queens may vent his frustrations by howling, fits of ill-temper, or masturbation.

A mature tom can be bred about every five days. If he must be used more often, the breeder can limit the number of matings with each queen to two or three rather than the dozen or more times that cats will breed if left together a day or two. In unusual cases, a tom might even be bred to two different females in the course of a single day, and is quite capable of impregnating both of them.

The tom's age

A precocious young male kitten can sire as early as six months. As with the queen, age of puberty varies with the breed, the shorthairs usually maturing much sooner than the longhairs. Most males will begin siring at ten to twelve months, though some may take sixteen months to mature and even longer depending on the season. Since a tom's sexual activity is greatest in the spring, a kitten born in late summer may not begin siring until his second spring. The prime breeding years for the tom are from his second birthday to his eighth, with some dropping off in the motility of the sperm in old age, though many fine old toms continue breeding their queens into old age.

It does no harm for a tom to be bred as soon as he is ready and willing, though there is some possibility of a queen's not conceiving due to a low motility in the sperm in a tom just reaching puberty. The tom should experience his first mating before his second birthday. Toms used extensively often have a haggard, unkempt appearance and in some breeds can lose color, so a young tom being shown might be bred only once or twice during his exhibition career as proof of his potency and willingness to breed.

Frequency of breeding the queen

A young queen of one to four years can bear more often than an older cat.

Two litters a year will not strain her resources; even three litters could be acceptable if the litters are small (one or two kittens) or if she should lose a litter. I remember visiting a home where a young queen had raised a single kitten. When I asked the owner if she would breed the queen again, she answered that she'd never breed any queen more than once a year — at which her fat, bored queen gave her a distinctly frustrated look, or so it seemed to me.

Naturally, frequency of breeding depends on the queen's health and condition. Nursing a litter to weaning age seems to take more out of many queens than does pregnancy itself. A queen who has lost her litter within a few days of birth will normally come into heat within a few days. Many breeders consider that this is an ideal time to breed her, assuming her weight and condition are good. An exception is the cat who has had a C-section; you will want to wait at least five months before breeding her again, and possibly longer.

Nursing queens will seldom come into heat as the production of milk inhibits the heat cycle. However, some may come into a strong heat when their milk supply begins to diminish after six to eight weeks. Unless she has raised a single kitten, you will want to allow more of a rest before breeding her again.

During illness a queen may not come into heat at all; however, keep her separate from your toms in case she does.

The queen's age

If kept with an entire male cat, the female kitten should be closely watched from about six months of age lest she come into heat and be mated prematurely. A tom will sometimes mount a female kitten, perhaps in play or because of "kitten heat" (not a true heat).

As a rule of thumb, a queen should not bear her first litter before her first birthday — which means she could be bred at about ten months. Many breeders consider it best to wait until the second heat; however, the novice breeder cannot always be certain of the first heat periods, which tend to be very undemonstrative compared to later heats.

A queen should not bear her first litter too late in life either: preferably before her second birthday, and without fail before her third. A breeder with an older queen that has not yet had her first litter should consult her vet.

The best rule for gauging a cat's age is this: the first year of life is equivalent to twenty human years, and each succeeding year is equivalent to seven human years. On her first birthday, therefore, a queen is in human terms a twenty-year-old, on her second birthday, twenty-seven, and on her third, thirty-four.

The prime bearing years for a queen are between her first and sixth birthdays. Beginning at age seven to nine there is generally a falling off in fertility, expressed in fewer pregnancies, more abortions and stillborn kittens, and fewer kittens per litter. At about age twelve many queens will no longer be able to reproduce. However, individuals vary enormously. Some queens continue bearing into their late teens, though only a single kitten per year may be produced. In practice, most breeders would probably stop breeding a queen when she approaches eight or nine years of age, if not sooner.

The effects of light on breeding cycles

The increasing proportion of daylight to dark hours in the early spring starts the breeding cycle. Laboratory tests in which queens were subject to about an equal number of daylight to dark hours have proven successful in bringing most queens into estrus. Some breeders have attempted to duplicate these results in order to bring their queens into heat during the off season, using artificial light and strictly controlling the hours. Whatever their reasons may be for doing so, such disruption of the normal biological cycle seems unwise, as does the use of artificial lighting, which has caused problems in reproductive abilities in some species. If your cats are strictly indoor animals, try to give them access to natural light throughout the year and particularly in the late winter. If you have more than one queen you may find that they cycle in exactly the same order each spring.

Planning the breeding schedule

Experienced breeders usually try to plan their breedings so that kittens are born at a convenient time. For example, if you work, you might hold a queen back a day or two to make it more likely that her kittens will be born on a weekend.

Breeders who show will always check their show calendars to be sure that kittening will not coincide with a show weekend. If it does, the queen should be held back until her next heat. Most queens come into heat so often that this is no problem.

Once you begin showing, you'll become aware of optimum times of year for kittens to be born from the standpoint of their show careers. For example, if you enjoy campaigning a kitten, you'll want to avoid "splitting" a show season. Kittens are shown for a four-month period between their fourth and eighth month birthdays. If a kitten is born on November 1, it will be four months old on March 1 and will have only two months to show of the current season, which ends April 30, and then two months in the new season, which begins May 1.

Females can be difficult to show because they begin losing coat and condition once they begin to cycle. You can possibly plan ahead for this problem by arranging her early adult show months – age eight to twelve months – for the time of year best for your area. That is, if most of the shows are between December and April, the optimum time for a female kitten to be born is May 1.

Finally, if you have a queen who gives birth easily but has trouble raising her kittens, you can time her breeding to coincide with that of another female who can then help raise both litters.

Stud service agreements

The following stud service agreements will apply both when you are in need of a stud and when you have a male yourself to offer at stud.

First, no serious breeder will accept unregistered queens to her stud. If she did so, she would be fostering the continued breeding of low-quality, non-registered kittens and opening herself to the criticism of other breeders. Nor should she accept poor quality queens, registered or not, since the stud's reputation can be damaged if a kitten from a poor litter is shown (both parents will be listed in the show catalog). However fine the stud, he cannot compensate for all the faults of a poor quality queen.

The best way to locate a good stud is through the breeder from whom you purchased your female kitten and at cat shows. Take a copy of your female's pedigree to a show and ask exhibitors how their lines might be expected to cross with your cat's. Your choice of stud will also be determined by convenience and cost. If possible, line up a second stud, since the one of choice may be otherwise occupied at the exact moment yours is howling for a mate. (Since cycles cannot be predicted accurately, it is impossible to reserve a stud's time in advance.) If a stud has been busy with another queen, he will need four or five days recovery time; meanwhile your queen may have gone off heat. The owner of the stud may sell him or neuter him, or the stud might be ill or even die, and the owner might forget to inform you until you call.

I would not take a maiden queen to a very expensive stud. Wait until she has proven herself with a healthy, sound litter before you invest a fortune in stud fees. Perhaps she will be one of those unfortunate queens that has only one kitten per litter, or she may be a poor mother. Know what to expect before you spend a lot of money.

Fees will vary with the quality and show record of the stud. An acceptable fee would be somewhat more than the price that one kitten from the litter could be expected to bring. For example, if kittens of your breed sell for an average of $200, a stud fee of $275 to $350 would be reasonable. If the stud is a Grand Champion, the kittens can be expected to bring more and the stud fee will be correspondingly greater.

A widely-used alternative is for the stud owner to take pick-of-litter. She will have to visit the breeder, send a representative, or choose a kitten from photographs before they have reached a salable age.

If you are the owner of a queen, don't count on the stud's owner wanting to take pick of litter. She may have too many kittens of her own or she may be uninterested in your queen's bloodlines. Then, too, while pick-of-litter seems an easy way out of the stud fee to many breeders, what if there's only one really nice kitten in the entire litter? What if that one kitten is really something special? It can hurt to watch such a kitten growing up, longing to show it, and knowing that the stud's owner will be by one day to carry it off.

A stud fee of $300 or more seems high to many novices, especially considering that the queen must be taken to the stud and all the stud's owner needs to do is put them together for a couple of days. But the stud fee should be thought of in a different light: the original cost and upkeep of the stud, the building of his special quarters, and the risk to him if the queen should turn nasty or if she harbors some infection. Despite the potential income from stud fees, the great majority of breeders keep a closed stud, i.e., breed only their own queens or those of good friends.

At the same time the stud fee is discussed, arrangements should be made for payment and provisions for the queen that does not become pregnant, loses her litter, or has only one surviving kitten. One commonly used arrangement is payment of half the fee when the queen is picked up after a successful mating and the other half when the kittens are born and past the danger stage of the first few days. The queen that does not become pregnant, aborts, or loses her litter would be returned at the next heat — usually after three weeks — and a third time if necessary. If the queen does not take from a proven stud, and at least three matings have been witnessed, I would say the stud's owner is justified in retaining the payment of some percentage of the stud fee for her trouble.

Some stud owners will guarantee only the queen's pregnancy in the belief that the stud has done his job and if the queen miscarries or loses her kittens at birth, it's not the stud owner's fault. A more understanding breeder would consider that litters are often lost through no fault of the queen's owner and would allow one or two free return stud services. It is also possible that the queen's owner will have only a single kitten for sale; the price it brings may not even pay for the stud fee, much less the time and expense of raising it. In such circumstances, the stud's owner might choose to keep only half the stud fee or she might allow a free return. Such contingencies should be discussed *in advance* and the agreement written out (a standard stud agreement form is given in the Appendix). A few stud owners will guarantee nothing more than that the tom mated the queen!

The stud's owner should insist on seeing the registration papers and a health certificate for a queen brought to her stud. She should demand in advance that the queen be clean and free of parasites and have her claws clipped. Some stud owners take it upon themselves to conduct an internal examination of the queen, resulting in possible injury or infection. Needless to say, this should never be done without the permission of the queen's owner, and the queen's owner shouldn't give it. If the stud's owner requires such an examination, a licensed veterinarian should do it.

A few people have disappeared with pregnant queens before paying the last half of the stud fee. Kittens born of such a mating can't be registered without the stud owner's signature; this is her protection. The escapee might attempt to falsify the registration papers or forge a signature, so the cat associations should be alerted by the stud's owner.

All sorts of problems arise over stud agreements, mostly due to misunderstandings. Proper planning and carefully written contracts will help prevent
them.

Offering your own tom at stud

Once you have your own stud, you will probably consider offering him at stud
as an easy way to make a little extra money. Well, it *isn't* easy, and can cost you
more in the long run than you can expect to make.

Who will be coming to your stud? That depends. Other breeders in your area
will have their own studs and will not be interested in using yours unless he is a
very successful show winner. And if he's *that* good, you probably won't want to
offer him at open stud (sell them kittens instead!).

The people coming to you for stud service will usually be very small breeders
with only one or two queens. A few may consider themselves serious breeders,
but most will only be interested in raising and selling a litter or two.

More often than not, their queens will be maidens, and a good percentage of
those will have grown up without other cats around. Nothing is more difficult
than getting such a queen bred – difficult and maybe impossible. First, the
queen may not even be in heat – many novices have trouble telling. If she *is* in
heat, she will probably be too frightened to show it. She's likely to be either
terrified or aggressive and may attack and injure your tom. At the very least,
she will frustrate him, as his persistent seduction techniques go completely
unrewarded. Meanwhile, you are feeding, boarding and cleaning up constantly.

If your tom *does* manage to breed the visiting queen, there's still no guarantee
that she will conceive. If she does conceive, she may still lose all or most of her
kittens, and you've gone to a lot of trouble for nothing.

Finally, you must remember that you are operating on trust – and you're sure
to run across those who will abuse that trust. What will you do if the queen's
owner informs you that she had no kittens, or lost them all? Go by her house in
the middle of the night and peer in the windows hoping to see something? If,
that is, she hasn't moved or given you a phony address. No, you just have to
take her at her word. You must also consider the risk of infection to your tom
and other cats.

On the other hand, you might be lucky and meet with nothing but honest
people with healthy, willing queens! But be prepared for problems.

Small versus large catteries

The small cattery is almost always an extension of pet ownership: perhaps
only one good queen, perhaps four or five cats. The advantages of such a very
small cattery: easily accommodated in your home, no major disruption of your
living patterns, no large amount of money tied up in breeding stock. The fact
that you will probably use outside stud service is both an advantage and a disadvantage: an advantage in that you will possibly have several studs to choose

from and can choose the one that will work best with your queen's lines (whereas those with their own stud feel obligated to use it, for reasons of economy, even though it may not be the best stud available for their queen); a disadvantage in that you are dependent on the stud's owner, must pay a stud fee, and must transport your queen to the stud. Another advantage of having a small cattery may not be immediately apparent: health problems, parasite problems and kitten mortality are usually much lower in the small cattery.

Disadvatages of the small cattery: primarily, that you cannot carry out a long-term breeding program without some assistance from other breeders; you can't keep many kittens to see how they will turn out; it is particularly hard to work with recessive colors and characteristics if you can only keep a few cats.

Mating

Since the tom is intensely territorial, the normal practice is for the queen to be brought to him. The queen's owner doesn't need to rush her there at the first sign of heat; there is no "best day" during the heat period at which she should be mated, for ovulation in the queen is induced by mating. Heat periods last from three days up to ten, so get your queen to the stud by the second or third day.

The queen should be placed in a cage inside or adjoining the stud's quarters so they can get to know each other. After several hours, or whenever the queen seems amenable to the idea, the two can be placed together and left to get on with it. In practice, the male and female are often placed together right from the start.

The breeding pair may discover love at first sight, or there may be hissing and spitting accompanied by flying fur. The main reason for failure to mate is that the queen is not truly in heat when brought to the male: the queen's owner may be so eager to get her bred that she mistakes a little tail-wagging for the flagging that signals true heat.

The stud's owner should supervise the mating and check on the cats from time to time, especially at the beginning. She must do her best to witness three completed matings, but some males are very shy around people so this may not be possible. Other males wouldn't care if the house were burning down around them and the queen was turned upside down: they'll get her bred come hell or high water. This the type of stud everyone wants.

If mating doesn't occur within twenty-four hours, it's probably a lost cause. The pair should be left together at least that long. They may mate every hour or so during that time. If the tom's services are going to be needed again within a few days, her owner may just want to allow the required three matings before separating him from the queen. Otherwise, it's best to leave them together for two or three days.

The queen invites the male by crouching down, hoisting her rump in the air and exposing her vulva, and treading with her hind legs while flagging her tail to one side. The male takes an interested sniff, calls to the queen and then grasps her firmly by the back of the neck while he mounts her. Penetration takes place for only a few seconds; then the queen cries out and tries to turn on the male, who jumps to one side. The male then washes his genitals while the queen rolls and rubs against the ground, with pauses for grooming. The process then begins again.

Interestingly, the male normally *cannot* mate unless he is able to grasp the queen's scruff in his teeth. This has led to some attempts at birth control in the form of a large collar for the queen's neck. However, males can learn to grasp the queen farther back, and this is essential for the small or short-bodied male.

Most cats are not very particular about their partners, but it does sometimes happen that a queen just does not like a particular tom and won't let him near her (but will greet the alleycat next door in raptures). An experienced and very aggressive male may get his way despite the queen's animosity, but a young or shy tom will give up in frustration. This can work the other way, too. A tom may take a dislike or disinterest in a particular queen.

Toms and queens who have mated before often recognize each other when reintroduced.

Cats are seldom injured during mating; when one is, it is almost always the tom. The tom seems to have a natural inhibition against harming the queen, while the queen has no such feelings. The toms that get hurt are those that haven't yet learned to be cautious, to approach from the rear and to wait until the queen signals her readiness. This is why the young tom should be given queens that are known to be kindly during mating for their first experience. In practice this is not always possible, and two raw beginners at the mating process will usually manage to sort everything out.

Injury to the queen, if any, usually consists of a few sores on the back of the neck or on the sides where a tom has been too enthusiastic in biting and treading.

Once the tom's owner has witnessed three matings, or is otherwise certain that the cats have mated, or that the cats are not going to mate, she will call the queen's owner to come pick up her cat. An exception might be made if the queen has been shipped a long distance; then the queen might be boarded until pregnancy is determined (about three weeks), or until she comes into heat again (also about three weeks). When a queen is boarded for more than a few days, the stud's owner might want to ask for compensation in addition to the stud fee. These boarding fees, if any, should be part of the original agreement.

The non-performing and infertile cat

The queen or tom that fails to produce when mated twice to proven producers should be examined by a vet. The cat may be too young or too old, in poor condition or overworked, or it may have some malformation of the genitals. The problem can also be psychological: the cat can be frightened by the sight of a stranger of his species, particularly if he has been raised in isolation. Time and proper care will correct many problems.

Other possible causes of infertility include infections, hormone imbalance, sterility, and genital malformation. Tests may include a blood count, a cervical culture and even surgical exploration of the uterus and ovaries. A really complete battery of tests can be very expensive, and may serve to only locate, but not remedy, the problem, so you must decide whether it would not be better to have the cat altered and kept as a pet.

The tom, if unproven, should be tried with at least two proven queens; some cats just aren't compatible. If he is inexperienced he may not even be "on target;" this problem is usually corrected by giving him a little time. A tom with an agreeable nature will sometimes allow his owner to help, either by steadying the queen or moving him into the proper position. But if you are in no doubt that he is siring, yet his queens do not settle, you must have him examined.

The tom over two years old who shows no interest in queens in heat may be suffering from a variety of psychological factors. He may be frightened by the sight of a strange queen, particularly if he's been raised in isolation. Such cats must have more time; they can regain their confidence if a potential mate is purchased as a kitten and allowed to grow up in the same house. Bear this in mind when buying your first kitten; buy two, or, if you can't afford it, adopt a nice domestic kitten so that your future breeder can develop social contact with another cat.

Conversely, the male can also be a victim of the "same old face" syndrome. He feels nothing but brotherly love towards the at-home queens, but give him a strange lovely and he's bursting with machismo. The tom can also tire of any queen after one or two days of almost constant mating; perhaps he gets fed up with being clobbered. The tom's owner shouldn't be concerned that he's lost his sexual drive when she sees the queen still in heat and the tom uninterested – provided, of course, that they've already mated several times.

A special case is the tom who is shut up continually in a small cage and loses all interest in his surroundings, including other cats. Though most toms must be caged, they should be given spacious quarters, lots of human contact, grooming, association with other cats throughout each day to keep their sparkle. No one who appreciates the special affection and vigor of the tom will be guilty of confining him to a miniscule cage in a dim basement room.

If the proven tom seems suddenly sterile, it's possible that he is being overused. Temporary infertility can also be a side-effect of certain drugs. Psychological factors – such as stress due to change in environment – can also be a factor, but they're more likely to be manifested in a refusal to breed than infertility.

The queen that fails to come into heat or has a very mild heat can be helped through reconditioning and vitamin therapy (Vitamin E has proven helpful to many breeders). Failing this, your veterinarian can prescribe medication that may bring her into heat. A course of contraceptives is usually followed by a strong heat when withdrawn.

Determining pregnancy

When your queen returns from the stud, or after she has been bred by your male, she may still show signs of heat and may even seem to come back into heat a few days later. This is not necessarily a sign that she did not conceive. However, if the queen definitely comes back into heat three weeks or more after the breeding and no evidence of conception is present, she should be returned to the male. Pregnant queens do occasionally come into heat about twenty-one days after mating; in this case you should be able to ascertain that she is pregnant, and you would not return her to the stud.

Check your queen's nipples. From fourteen to eighteen days after conception, they will begin to enlarge and turn a bright pink, where before they were tiny and pale pink, almost white in maiden queens. At three weeks you can gently palpate the queen's abdomen; the kittens can be felt as little marble-sized lumps. However, if you're not used to palpating cats, you may not be certain that what you feel are the kittens. A vet or experienced breeder could help you, and even make a good guess at the number she's carrying. Later on, the kittens grow together into a mass and cannot be felt distinctly.

Around the sixth week the abdomen becomes definitely swollen and the outline of the kittens can be felt. Maiden queens can outfox you, though, by hardly swelling at all.

By the eighth and final week you'll be able to feel the kittens moving within the queen's belly. A queen full of healthy, vigorous kittens will feel like a sack of potatoes during her last week, and you can sit next to her and see the babies squirming under her flank.

It is not necessarily a sign of trouble if the kittens are *not* real kickers, and you shouldn't worry if at times you can detect no movement; even unborn kittens must sleep.

Some veterinarians recommend vaccinating all pregnant queens with the killed enteritis vaccine about two weeks before the kittens are due to maximize the antibodies that the kittens will receive at birth through the mother's milk. However, most recommend avoiding any type of vaccine, drug, or worming medications during pregnancy. The relationship of certain drugs with kitten mortality or malformation is firmly established. Other products have been safely tested, but are still best avoided. The prohibition on drugs and live vaccines should extend if possible to those cats with which the queen comes in contact.

Final preparations for kittening

During the last week before parturition is expected, if not earlier, get the queen used to confinement in the area you've chosen for the maternity room.

Most people use a bedroom, as I do. If you must sit up all night attending the birth of kittens, you might as well do where you're most comfortable. Raising the kittens in your bedroom also allows you to keep close track of their progress.

The kittening box is a big cardboard box, a new one each time to avoid the growth of infections. (You can also use a plastic crate or a carrier).Cut a hole into one side of the box about three inches from the bottom, big enough for the queen to get through. This entrance will keep the kittens inside the box until they are old enough to climb over the side (about two and one-half weeks). It will also help prevent drafts, and is a better means of access for the queen than jumping over the side, which could injure her tender nipples. The box is stood inside its own lid set sideways to the ground, thus forming a partial top for it. A towel is draped over the opening at the top. This gives the queen a dimly lit, private "cave" of her own; it also allows you to look inside easily by lifting the towel or sliding the box out.

The box is carpeted with many layers of newspapers torn into pieces. The queen may get into the box and dig around during the last few days, or she may ignore it completely. At the least, she becomes accustomed to its presence.

The whole room should be cozily heated to about seventy degrees. Any disinfectants, flea powders, or strong cleaning agents should be avoided in the kittening room during the two weeks before parturition.

For about the last five days before kittening, massage the queen's nipples for a few minutes, using a little olive oil on the tip of your finger. Your queen will have at least eight nipples, possibly ten, and you must check them all to be sure they are clean and not caked or cracked. The olive oil will soften the nipples and forces the queen to be attentive to them. Older queens often have a protective waxy substance on their nipples. Do not attempt to remove it, for the olive oil will soften it and the queen will remove it herself by licking. If any nipple is cracked, abcessed or seems abnormally swollen, call your vet at once. It is essential that the newborn kittens not be allowed to nurse from a torn or scratched nipple. Sometimes a nipple can be bandaged securely to prevent its being suckled.

If your cat's hair is extremely long, carefully trim away some of the hair right around the nipples so that the kittens can find them easily. Also trim away the hair around the vagina and back legs. A longhair queen sometimes seems so distressed at the messiness of giving birth that she tries to clean herself and ignores the kittens. Also, a kitten or afterbirth can get tangled up in the very long pantaloons of some longhairs. If your queen is very swollen you should also help keep her clean, since she may be unable to wash her hindquarters.

Finally, if the queen has fleas or is dirty, give her a bath now. If you use a flea dip or powder, rinse very thoroughly around her nipples so the newborns will not ingest any.

Are all these preparations really necessary? Surely queens have been giving birth for thousands of years without man's help? True — but many have died for lack of help, or lost their kittens. "Instinct" is nebulous and fallible, and to depend on it is irresponsible. Instinct cannot help if something goes seriously wrong, but *you* can.

The kittening kit

Once the queen and the kittening area have been prepared, the last step is to get out the kittening kit. It should contain:

(1) Your vet's phone number, home phone number, and an emergency 24-hour number. Arrange with your vet *in advance* what you should do in an emergency. If you're not sure what constitutes an emergency, discuss this as well. Should you need to take the queen to him — which is unlikely — you have the box ready and need only drop the lid over it, or you can move her to a carrier.

(2) Cotton balls, gauze pads, or tissues, for helping to clean off the queen and kittens.

(3) Paper towels for picking up any messy remnants.

(4) A few paper bags for disposing of wet bedding, dirty tissues, afterbirths, or stillborn kittens.

This small kit will carry you through the first few litters of kittens. As you become more experienced at cat midwifery, you may want to add some of the following items, which, while not strictly necessary, you may find helpful at times.

(1) Hemostats, scissors, and cold sterilizer, for breaking the umbilical cord if the queen fails to do it herself. These are optional, because you *can* pinch and shred the cord with your fingernails if necessary.

(2) An aspirator, for kittens that do not breathe right away, to draw fluids from the mouth and throat. There are several alternative methods that will be discussed later.

(3) A warm towel, heated in the oven, and a small box or shoebox. You can also keep the towel warm on a heating pad or hot water bottle. You will remove the kittens one by one, wrap them in the warm towel to dry and keep them out of the way until the queen has finished giving birth. This prevents the first-born kittens from being crushed or pushed into a chilly corner while the mother gives birth to the subsequent kittens; it also gives them a chance to recover and avoid expending energy in fruitlessly crawling around the nest.

Remember: when you're starting out to learn the mechanics of kittening, your first rule should be to interfere as little as possible until you know what to expect from a normal birth, and when a dangerous situation may be developing. As you gain experience, you'll be able to help the queen more and more.

Illness and abortion during pregnancy

False pregnancy, abortion, illness and changed behaviour during pregnancy are all unusual in the cat, as is difficulty in kittening.

Vomiting is occasionally seen in the queen during the last two weeks of pregnancy. A large litter can occupy so much space in the abdomen that the stomach is squashed and can't accommodate its normal volume of food. It's a good idea, therefore, to feed the pregnant queen three or four small meals a day, and leave dry food out for nibbling. If the vomiting does not clear up or if other signs of illness are apparent, have her checked by your vet.

A fat queen should not be overfed during pregnancy; in fact, it will do no harm if she loses a little weight before kittening. Overweight can result in reduced fertility and difficult delivery. The best course to follow is to trim your queens down before breeding. Ovid made this recommendation two thousand years ago for all breeding animals: "Keep them lean and spare."

If you need to take a pregnant queen for a checkup, make a note of the date of breeding before you leave home. X-rays may be necessary and are considered safe for the unborn kittens during the last weeks before kittening.

False pregnancies, common in dogs, are rare in cats. Sometimes an obviously-swollen queen suddenly thins down and the breeder may think she has had a false pregnancy. While this could be the case, she might also have miscarried and eaten all the evidence.

Approaching signs of kittening

You can't be sure how to interpret your queen's behaviour prior to kittening until she has produced a litter or two. There are so many variables that the following description should be read in general terms.

Gestation in the cat ranges from fifty-nine days to seventy-three days, with sixty-three to sixty-five days being the average. Beginning with her second litter, a queen's gestation period tends to be the same for each subsequent litter, so this will give you an idea of when to look for first-stage labor.

First stage labor lasts from one hour to twenty-four, and will be obvious in most, though not all, queens that are closely watched. The queen becomes restless, constantly demands attention, scratches around in her nest or elsewhere, and may have some vaginal discharge of a yellowish color. Some of these signs can be seen several days before kittening, and I have sat up many a night in vain, only to see the queen doze off contentedly at dawn. The discharge is an almost certain sign that kittening will start within several hours. There may be no discharge at all, or the queen may lick it away unobserved, so it does no good to be constantly peering under her tail!

Usually a queen's temperature will drop about two degrees within twenty-four hours of parturition. Some breeders take advantage of this fact by taking the queen's temperature morning and evening. If you want to do this, be sure to start well in advance so that you know what your queen's normal temperature is: as in everything else, there's considerable variation from one cat to the next. Write down the times and figures until you are familiar with the queen's normal fluctuations. What you are looking for is a sudden drop in temperature that is *not* part of the normal pattern. When this occurs – even though the subsequent reading shows a normal temperature, look for the kittens to appear within twenty-four hours.

If you are a working person, try to come home during your lunch hour to check on your queen. If this is impossible, console yourself with the thought that kittening usually takes place at night, and that a queen with kindly feeling towards humans will often wait until her benefactor is present — mine all do. Should kittening take place without your help, the queen will probably get through it on her own if she is not a maiden. In some species, such as the horse, if something goes wrong it goes wrong fast. Fortunately for cat breeders, feline problems in parturition usually take some time to develop.

However, you should make *every effort* to be at hand for your queen's kittening.

As the queen approaches kittening, sit by the nest and encourage her to stay inside, but don't force her. You'll have time to move her to the box when the first contractions start, when she'll be too preoccupied to resist.

First-time mothers may try to leave the nest in between kittens, possibly in an attempt to escape the strange odors, wetness and pain. Reassure her and try to keep her in the box. But if she is about to panic, let her have the kittens where she will and then move them, and her, to the box. Make sure there is nowhere in the room inaccessible to you, or she will surely have her babies in that spot!

Kittening

Besides keeping a close watch and reassuring the queen, your main job will be to pick out the wet and bloody pieces of newspaper. Of course you mustn't disturb the queen as you do this, but she will naturally circle around in the box and whenever she moves you can pick out the big, sodden masses (don't worry about getting *all* of it). The queen will be more comfortable and the kittens will dry faster. You should have enough papers in the nest that you're still left with a good layer when you're finished.

The first kitten is preceded by a large, dark sack of fluid resembling a huge grape. This will be licked away by the queen. The kitten follows, forced out in a few minutes by the strong, regular contractions, though it may take up to half an hour of straining. Sometimes the queen will groan, growl or even scream as the kitten slides out.

The kitten might come out enclosed in a shining wet sack, kicking and gasping inside it. Often the sack has already been torn during the kitten's passage through the vagina. You must make sure that the sack is broken and that the kitten is breathing. Pinch the sack around the newborn's mouth and tear it open; then dry around and inside the mouth with a small tissue. This takes only a few seconds, and you should be able to do it without taking the kitten from the nest. In fact, you will *have* to, because the afterbirth may still be inside the queen.

If the queen is bending over her newborn and you cannot see whether or not it is breathing, listen for the tiny squeak. There are kittens so vigorous that they're screaming lustily before they hit the ground. Others sound as though they're underwater. No matter: they're breathing. If, after a few moments, you can't hear the kitten squeak or see it breathing, you must move the mother aside if necessary and make sure the kitten is breathing.

Some breeders will take each kitten at this point and shake it upside down or even place it in an oxygen tent. Neither of these practices is recommended for the novice, who's likely to do more harm than good, unless of course the kitten is still not breathing (discussed below).

Besides picking out the papers, clean off the kitten and queen with cotton balls or tissues if this doesn't disturb the mother. Sometimes the queen is preoccupied with herself and ignores the kitten. Sometimes two kittens slide into the world almost simultaneously. By massaging the newborn you help dry it off and also strengthen the breathing pattern. Don't be overly gentle: watch how vigorously the queen licks her babies, and imitate her.

If the queen is tending to her latest-born, you may just as well leave her alone until she starts straining for the birth of the next. She will then turn away from the newborn and you can safely remove it and wrap it loosely inside a warm towel with its brothers and sisters. You can also make a quick examination for deformities and to determine sex at this time.

You *can* leave all the kittens in the nest, but the mother might lie or step on them. They will certainly be in her way, and their efforts to nurse will be fruitless as the queen circles around in the box. When kittening is complete, or if there is a long respite between births, you can put the babies, now warm and dry, back with their mother, and place each one gently on a nipple.

The umbilical cord and afterbirth

While watching your queen's kittening, don't be so absorbed by the newborns that you forget the rest of the process. Try to count the afterbirths, one for each kitten, and call your vet the next day if you think one was retained as this can be a source of infection. Twin kittens (two kittens to one afterbirth) are not unknown. If twin kittens have white spotting, the spots will be mirror images.

The queen may deliver kitten and afterbirth together, or the kitten may come first, followed several minutes later, after a bit of straining, by the afterbirth. If the queen gets up and moves around before delivering the afterbirth, try not to let the kitten be dragged by its umbilical cord. You could pick it up and move it gently with the mother, or you could cut the cord yourself. It's always better to wait a few minutes before cutting the cord, because blood will continue to flow through the cord to the kitten after birth. And if you cut the cord while the placenta is still inside the queen, it may not be delivered later. You can try pulling *very gently* on the cord; sometimes the placenta will just slide out easily.

If it doesn't come easily, leave it alone. The placenta at the other end may be caught behind the next kitten and will come out after its birth. Wait for it to be delivered naturally.

Once the afterbirth is delivered, the queen will eat it and then chew down the cord until she bites it off about an inch from the kitten's belly. I've heard of queens that keep going and eat the kitten too, or parts of it, but I've never see this happen. If the placenta is not attached to the kitten the queen may show no interest in it; lift it out and dispose of it.

It should not be necessary to treat the umbilical cord. If the nest is kept warm and dry, the cord will shrivel up quickly and drop off about three days after birth. Check the cord at birth and daily thereafter for any sign of wetness or infection.

Some breeders will not allow the queen to eat the afterbirth, or only the first one or two, because of a mild diarrhea that can result from eating them all. In the wild state, a queen eats the afterbirths to keep her nest clean and to provide herself with vital nourishment at a time when she can't hunt effectively. A few queens will not be interested in the snack. Simply remove the afterbirth and the kitten too, of course, if still attached.

If the cord is unbroken and if you've waited a few minutes for blood to continue flowing to the kitten, remove both kitten and afterbirth from the nest, one in each hand. Place them on your lap on a warm towel. Pinch the cord about an inch from the kitten's belly for a few minutes and then shred it with your fingers, being careful not to pull against the kitten. If you prefer to cut the cord, first massage the cord along its length in the direction of the kitten. Then use hemostats to clamp the cord. The serrated teeth will pinch the cord together more effectively than you could do with your fingers. Wait a minute or two, and then cut next to the hemostats, or shred the cord with your fingers, on the side *away* from the kitten. Remove the hemostats. There should be very little bleeding.

If the mother has bitten the cords, some will be long and some short; this isn't important. The cords should start to dry up almost at once. Check them daily to be sure they are dry. If there's any sign of wetness, dust them with antibiotic powder and consult your vet if necessary. Infections can enter quite easily through the cord.

The cords will fall off at about three days. You'll find them dry, hard, and shrivelled in the box. If the cords are still attached when the kittens are a week old, but otherwise appear normal (dry and shrivelled), try twisting them gently, but do not pull directly against the kitten. If they still don't come off, cut the cord very close to the body, then leave it alone.

When to call the vet

Vets are used to getting panic calls in the middle of the night when kittening is proceeding quite normally, so when you call be ready with the facts. The following problems would all necessitate an immediate call:

(1) Regular, strong contractions prolonged for more than a half hour. There may be a kitten, possibly a dead one, stuck in the birth canal and the queen's life will be endangered if she is allowed to sap all her strength in a futile attempt to deliver it.

(2) A small part of a kitten keeps appearing and disappearing with the queen's contractions; attempt to help her yourself before calling the vet.

(3) Sudden hemorrhaging of the queen. A certain amount of blood is a normal accompaniment to birth, but a large or continuous flow is a danger signal. You must get help fast.

(4) The queen delivers one or two kittens and then stops, though she obviously has kittens left. You must distinguish here between a cat in real trouble — in which case she needs emergency treatment — and one that's just taking a break. Cats can rest up to twelve hours in between kittens, although this is very unusual. If the queen is resting comfortably, wait until normal office hours before calling your vet. If she's in obvious distress, call at once.

(5) An afterbirth not delivered. This, too, can wait for normal office hours if the queen is otherwise well.

It is *useless* to make an emergency call for a kitten that is born dead or dying. Unless you can get to the vet within a few minutes, there is no hope for the kitten. The vet can do little more for a newborn than you can do yourself.

When you ask your vet about emergency care prior to kittening, ask him to read over this list. If he knows you are well prepared, he'll be that much more willing to help you in case of trouble.

The partially-delivered kitten

The normal birth position for most mammals is belly-down and head first, with front legs stretched out alongside the head. In cats, breech births — hind end first — are just as common, and not to be feared. However, it's most often a breech birth when the queen gives up on a partially-delivered kitten. A kitten will usually be stuck at the shoulders, its widest part. Since half the kitten is delivered, you can grasp it firmly and pull it out, using a downward motion and short, side-to-side jerks. Have someone hold the queen if possible or she may turn on you in pain. If she is still contracting, time your pulls to her contractions. Sometimes turning the kitten about a quarter-turn will help.

If the kitten and vaginal opening are dry, use a little Vaseline or baby oil as a lubricant on both. Be sure to grasp the kitten's entire body surface when you pull, and never pull on just the legs. You can also try pushing the kitten very gently back inside and trying to reposition it.

If just a leg or two legs keep appearing and then disappearing, try to determine if they are front legs or back legs. The kitten may be twisted sideways. If this seems to be the case, tie a bit of cloth around the leading leg and try to work the other end of the kitten back. It's difficult to get a finger very far into the birth canal, though it can be done. You can try to massage the kitten into position through the queen's flanks. Use a little common sense and you should be able to solve most problems that arise. But don't become so involved in aiding the newborn that you forget the queen. If she is on the point of collapse or in great pain, call your emergency service at once.

The kitten that won't breathe

Give the queen a few minutes to wash the kitten clean. If she doesn't, or if she stops before the kitten has taken its first breath, dry around the mouth and then massage the kitten vigorously. The kitten will start to gasp, then breathe spasmodically, and finally settle into a normal breathing pattern.

But if your massage has no effect, you must take the kitten from the nest. If the afterbirth has been delivered and is still attached, remove that as well. Breathing comes first, and the cord can be attended to later. If the afterbirth is still inside the queen, you must cut the cord first before you can remove the kitten.

Some breeders will swing the kitten, enclosed between their palms, in an arc with arms outstretched. This is supposed to remove fluids and shock the kitten into breathing. If you try this, be sure that the kitten's head is supported as well as its body, or you could snap its neck. I've had little success with this method.

Some kittens can be saved with mouth-to-mouth resusitation. Clean around and inside the mouth, very gently, with tissue. If you have an aspirator (available from your vet or from vet-supply houses), slide it gently a little way down the throat and then suck up any fluids that have accumulated. If you don't have an aspirator, just suck *in* before you start mouth-to-mouth, and spit the fluids out.

With the kitten on its back, hold its mouth open with two fingers and place your own mouth over its entire muzzle. Use tiny breaths when you breath into the kitten: its lung capacity is small. Hold two fingers of one hand on the kitten's ribcage and press very gently down to expel each breath. Do not give up too soon! It can take two or three minutes to revive a kitten. I have never failed to start a kitten breathing that I knew was alive at birth. Some kittens, however, will be stillborn. If you're not certain, make every effort, for giving up will certainly be fatal.

The chilled kitten

Perhaps you return home one afternoon to discover that your queen has delivered her kittens without your aid. Search the area carefully for kittens that may have been born outside the nest. Such kittens might be limp and cold to the touch, but they are not necessarily dead; their breathing may be shallow and imperceptible. In mountaineering medicine, we are taught that no one is ever cold and dead until he is *warm* and dead. The same applies to the chilled kitten.

Heat a towel at once in the oven or in a pan on top of the stove and wrap the kitten in it. The towel should be *hot*, not just warm (but don't attempt to hasten matters by putting the kitten itself in the oven). Alternatively, you can place the kitten in a bowl of hot water, holding its head out so that it can breathe. The kitten should revive after a few minutes of warming, and will be none the worse for its chill. If ten minutes or more of warming have no effect, the kitten is dead.

Stillborn and deformed kittens

Stillborn kittens are common in the cat. Deformed kittens will occasionally be seen, and the breeder should not be too quick to put the blame for them on her bloodlines or on inbreeding, unless the same problem continually recurs. Nor should the breeder be ashamed to admit that her cats have produced a deformed kitten: all species are subject to natal deformities, including our own.

Kinked tails can vary from a tiny notch to a tail twisted back upon itself. Although associated with the Siamese (many people think a Siamese is *supposed* to have a kinked tail), it can occur in any breed. The condition is strictly cosmetic, and in some breeds part of the show standard, such as the Manx and Japanese Bobtail.

Cleft palate is another common deformity in cats. In the past, such kittens died because they could not nurse properly. There is now a simple operation to correct the condition, depending on severity. The kitten should be placed in a pet home and not used for breeding, for cleft palate is thought to be hereditary. Check every newborn for cleft palate; it must be corrected at once, for the kitten will be unable to nurse effectively.

Extra toes are also fairly common. Such cats are called *polydactyls*, meaning many-toed. This condition can go unobserved in the very young kitten. Such a cat cannot be shown and should not be used for breeding, though it will otherwise lead a normal life. The deformity is actually attractive to some buyers, and the basis of a psuedo-breed.

An umbilical hernia, where part of the kitten's intestines are enclosed in a pouch outside the kitten's stomach, can often be corrected by a vet, who will push the intestine back inside and close the gap with a few stitches.

Twisted limbs are sometimes seen, with feet or legs bent backwards or folded over. These are very often just caused by the kitten's position in the uterus, where some obstruction, another kitten or the ribcage, for example, has prevented a limb from developing in the normal direction. Do not put down an otherwise healthy kitten with twisted limbs, as these will usually straighten out on their own within about two weeks after birth. If they don't come into the proper position on their own, see if your vet can make a tiny cast to pull the limb into the proper place.

Other deformities will not be apparent till later in life: the absence of one or both testicles, for example. There might also be deformities of internal organs or the nervous system that can cause death, though no sign is outwardly visible.

Occasionally a fetus will die before it is fully developed. It might be expelled at once or carried full-term and delivered normally. The delivery of such fetuses can be accompanied by the birth of quite normal kittens. A completely developed kitten that is stillborn may have died in the uterus or just before birth. A maiden queen's very first kitten is sometimes stillborn, perhaps due to its difficult passage through the as yet unstretched birth canal.

You're certain to be concerned when your queen gives birth to stillborn or deformed kittens. The cause of such problems is almost always impossible to determine: heredity, abnormal embryonic development, poor nutrition and faulty uterine environment can all be factors. Over some of these factors the breeder has no control whatsoever. Therefore, you should not be unduly worried over an occasional deformity or stillbirth. An exception to this should be made, however: if the same deformity occurs several times, or if it is obviously related to some form of extreme breeding, you should re-examine your breeding program and ask those people working with the same bloodlines if they have seen the problem. Too many breeders hush up any and all problems for fear that their bloodlines will become anathema. They are doing the breed itself a disservice. No one is breeding cats in isolation.

Take a deformed kitten to your vet. He will know if the condition can be corrected surgically, and if not, he can save you the trauma of killing the kitten yourself.

C-Sections

If a queen in labor has reached an impasse, or if the pregnant queen has not gone into labor on schedule, consult your veterinarian. If manipulations and drugs cannot bring on or complete kittening, he will perform a C-section.

An xray may be taken first to determine the number and placement of the kittens. After anesthetizing the queen, an incision is made in her lower belly or sometimes the flank, the uterus is also incised and the kittens removed. Since the kittens will have been anesthetized along with their mother, efforts must be made to revive them. Usually at least a portion of the litter will be lost.

However, the queen normally recovers quickly and is able to raise her litter, although she may not produce any milk, so the breeder must be prepared to hand-feed the babies.

Queens that have required a C-section should not be bred again for at least six months to allow the uterus to heal completely. Unless a physical deformity prevented natural birth, the likelihood of her requiring another C-section is no greater than that of any other cat.

The cost of a C-section runs around $225.

Litter size

An average litter consists of four kittens. Shorthairs will generally have larger litters, longhairs smaller litters. Litter size is often the same for each queen. Some may have only one or two on a regular basis; other may have six or seven each time. Nine or ten is a very large litter and thirteen or more approaches the all-time record. It's to be hoped that the queen's litter will be around the average, since the newborns in a very large litter may be extremely tiny and frail. If all live — which is doubtful — the queen's resources will be severely strained by all those hungry mouths. One or two is equally bad, since it limits the number you have to select from for your breeding program, not to mention how many you will have for sale. In addition, a queen that carries only one or two kittens may have trouble at birth, since the kittens tend to be larger than in a normal-size litter.

Litter size is determined by the number of eggs ovulated and it will make little difference if you change males. Recent research has shown that as many as thirty eggs are actually fertilized, but most of the embryos are reabsorbed almost at once. The number that develop to full term seems to depend on environmental factors.

Some breeders have tried to influence litter size by resorting to drugs. This may endanger the queen and perpetuate the problem, since litter size is partly hereditary. When buying a female kitten, ask the breeder about litter size. If your kitten's mother tended to have normal-sized litters, she probably will also. Remember when buying a kitten for breeding that fertility is just as important as the more immediately visible features.

Litter size will fall off when a queen approaches old age — say at around eight years — and finally taper off into a single kitten a year, more stillbirths, more abortions, and finally no more pregnancies. Some queens, however, continue to produce a kitten or two a year well into old age.

Size of the kittens

You might want to keep a growth chart for at least one or two litters of kittens, recording weight at birth and daily gain for each individual. Weigh each at the same time daily and be careful to differentiate between kittens. A small postage scale is cheap and will indicate half-ounces. A more finely-determined, larger capacity scale, though quite expensive, is useful not only for kittens but for weighing food and your mail as well, so you may want to splurge.

Weight at birth is dependent on breed, number of kittens in the litter, state of health, and position in the uterus. In a large litter the variation may be enormous, with the biggest kitten weighing in at twice the weight of the smallest. The tiniest kittens may weigh just one ounce; the largest, almost five ounces. These extremes are unusual: a normal weight is two to three ounces.

Don't assume that the smallest "runt" kittens are going to become weakly or undersized cats. Very often they catch up and even surpass their littermates in size and strength, though it may take them months to do so. During the first few weeks, the weight ratio between kittens will probably be maintained.

In weighing the kittens you are looking for a steady rate of growth in each one. There is often no gain until the second or third day after birth, but there should be no initial weight *loss* either. Generally each kitten will gain from one-quarter to one-half ounce daily. Birth weight will be doubled at the end of the first week, and tripled at the end of the second.

A significant or continual weight loss for any one kitten is of course a danger signal, but in practice is seen long after the other signs that mark an ailing kitten.

Growth Chart of a Typical Litter

Days of age	Kitten 1	Kitten 2	Kitten 3	Kitten 4	Kitten 5
Newborn	2 oz	3 oz	4 oz	3 oz	1¾ oz
One	2½ oz	3 oz	4 oz	3 oz	2 oz
Two	2¾ oz	3½ oz	4½ oz	3½ oz	2¼ oz
Three	2½ oz	3½ oz	5 oz	4 oz	2¾ oz
Four	2¾ oz	4 oz	5½ oz	4½ oz	3½ oz
Five	2¾ oz	4½ oz	6 oz	4½ oz	3 oz
Six	3½ oz	5 oz	5¾ oz	4¾ oz	3¼ oz
Seven	3¾ oz	5 oz	6¼ oz	5½ oz	3¼ oz
Eight	3¼ oz	5¼ oz	6¾ oz	5¾ oz	3¼ oz
Nine	3½ oz	5¾ oz	7 oz	6½ oz	3½ oz
Ten	3¾ oz	5¾ oz	7 oz	7 oz	4 oz
Eleven	4½ oz	6½ oz	8 oz	7 oz	4½ oz
Twelve	5 oz	6½ oz	8 oz	7¾ oz	4½ oz
Thirteen	5¼ oz	7 oz	8½ oz	8 oz	5¼ oz
Fourteen	5¾ oz	7¾ oz	8½ oz	8½ oz	5¾ oz
Fifteen	6 oz	8¼ oz	9 oz	9 oz	6 oz
Sixteen	7 oz	8¼ oz	9½ oz	9 oz	6¼ oz
Seventeen	7¼ oz	8¾ oz	9½ oz	9½ oz	6½ oz
Eighteen	7½ oz	9 oz	10½ oz	10 oz	6¾ oz
Nineteen	7¾ oz	9½ oz	11½ oz	10¾ oz	7¼ oz
Twenty	8¼ oz	10½ oz	12 oz	11½ oz	7¼ oz
Twenty-One	9 oz	10½ oz	13 oz	12 oz	8½ oz

Note that the kittens maintained the same relative weights throughout these first weeks, the smallest ones very gradually "catching up." However, even the smallest grew into a normal-sized cat. Note also the occasional, though temporary, loss of weight. This could also be due to time weighed (whether before or after nursing).

The healthy kitten

A healthy newborn has a firm feel and well-directed movements. Although it may take some time to locate a productive nipple, once it does the kitten latches on securely. If the mother should get up, the kittens sometimes cling so strongly that they hang from her belly like little sausages. The healthy kitten spends about a third of its time nursing, in bouts of ten to forty-five minutes, and the rest of its time sleeping. The kittens often nurse in shifts, so don't assume that a kitten sleeping while its littermates nurse is necessarily sick.

The healthy newborn seldom cries except when its mother leaves the nest, and then it emits a piercing, high-pitched squeal that brings the mother hurrying back.

When they're ready to sleep, the kittens arrange themselves in a little stack for warmth, sleeping head to flank or one on top of the other. Every few minutes the healthy kitten will twitch and perhaps make suckling motions. This twitching often worries the novice breeder, while in fact it is the surest mark of good health.

Another mark of the healthy kitten is the "curl-up" reflex, usually present by the second day after birth and continuing on until long after the kittens are weaned. If you hold the kitten by its head and let the body hang down, after a few seconds the kitten will draw his hind legs up towards his body and bring his tail up between his legs as though curling into a ball. He will also become very still and passive.

In the wild state, the curl up reflex keeps the kitten still and prevents the hind legs from dragging across the ground in the mother's way should she need to carry it. Its remnants are seen even in the adult cat, who will often become passive and stop struggling when grasped at the scruff of the neck.

The kitten's belly is not necessarily an indicator of health. Some kittens will be getting so much milk that their tummies are stretched tight as a drum. Others have a softer, almost slack belly. However, they are not necessarily ill. Kittens can survive on less than the optimum amount of milk. I have done experiments in mixing litters and found that the kittens placed on "super-mom" will, after three weeks, weigh more than twice as much as kittens from the same litter, with the same birth-weight, left on their mother. The kittens are much smaller – their growth rate has adjusted to the smaller milk supply – but otherwise healthy, and they eventually grow into normal-sized cats.

The ailing kitten

The ailing kitten has a mushy feel to its body. It will feel cool to the touch. Rather than stacking up in a pile with the rest of the litter, it may lie by itself and will not twitch and squirm during sleep like its healthier littermates.

It will usually show signs of dehydration. The skin will be loose and slack, rather than tight and elastic. If you pull up a bit of skin, it stays up rather than snapping back into place. (A kitten may be *born* with a slack, wrinkled skin, but health and an adequate milk supply should relieve the condition within ten or twelve hours.)

When you test the curl up reflex, it will dangle limply from your hand.   The mother will ignore the ailing kitten, sometimes pushing it into a corner of the nest while she tends to the others. Very rarely, she will eat it.

These signs may be apparent two to four days after birth. If you are certain that a kitten is sick, remove it from the nest – it is getting no attention anyway – and wrap it in a towel placed on a heating pad set on low, in such a way that it cannot escape. If you want to try to save the kitten, tube feed glucose solution and inject electrolytes under the skin (get them from your vet), massage it regularly and treat it like an orphan. If it reaches the point where it will nurse from a bottle, put it back with the others at once. Use glucose solution instead of formula at first because the sick and dehydrated kitten needs energy, not protein. When the kitten starts improving, change to formula.

You will probably not save the ailing kitten if it's under a week old. Once you've noticed that it is ailing, it will probably die within twenty-four hours, a little longer if you're trying to save it.

The great majority of newborn deaths proceed in the above manner. Sometimes, though, you'll find that a fat and healthy kitten suddenly dies within the span of the couple of hours. Even more rarely, a queen will accidentally lie upon and smother a newborn kitten.

The problem mother

Almost all queens are excellent mothers. For the first twenty-hour hours after birth the queen should stay with her kittens constantly. She'll be thirsty from her labors, so offer her a dish of warm milk or formula after she gives birth, right in the nest (don't leave it there or the kittens will crawl in it). If the queen leaves her newborns, or moves them from spot to spot, or appears uncomfortable when they try to nurse, you must examine both her and her nest.

If the nest big enough for her to lie stretched-out comfortably? Is the bottom well padded with dry papers? Is the box, or the room, too hot for her comfort? Did the queen expel all afterbirths? Can you feel one or two kittens still inside her abdomen? Are her nipples soft and functional?

Try folding a pillowcase and putting this over the papers in the box. Try making a new box. Try placing the box in one corner of your bed. Try arranging pillows, blankets and towels in a corner of your bed to form a nest. As a last resort, shut both kittens and mothers into a large portable cage in your room. The cage must be large enough to allow her to escape from her kittens (i.e., lie down outside the nest).

If the queen persists in ignoring her babies or seems to be on the verge of harming them, you must take them away and place them with another queen or raise them as orphans. The rare queen who behaves this way will often settle down into motherhood with her second litter. If she doesn't, have her spayed and keep her as a pet, or find her a pet home. I know of a breeder who had a cat put down because she ate her newborn kittens, and felt this "punishment" was justified. The cat was quite nice in other respects and would have made a lovely pet for somebody. Do not blame the cat if its instincts go awry.

Simultaneous litters and other cats

If you have more than one queen, it's a good idea to plan your litters together. Then if one queen has a huge litter, you can distribute kittens to another, and if one queen rejects her kittens, or becomes ill or even dies at birth, the whole lot can be placed with a different mother.

When transferring kittens from one mother to another, for whatever reason, use some care. For up to forty-eight hours after birth the queen will nurse just about anything and everything. But once she learns the smell and sound of her own kittens she may reject the newcomer.

If you have several litters due, it's best to separate each one until the kittens are up and around at about three weeks of age, at which point most queens will not care which kittens are hers. If you want to keep two litters together, watch carefully to make sure that neither mother objects. Queens that are good friends will nurse each other's kitten indiscriminately, and even share the same nest.

Many tom cats are excellent fathers, though this is not supposed to be natural in the cat, where the wild mother must raise her young alone. Your tom, or other pet cats, will naturally by curious about the kittens and there's no reason why they shouldn't share in the fun of raising a litter – under your supervision, of course, and providing the mother does not object. My own toms will wash and cuddle the babies, though they're always taken aback when the little ones start searching for a nipple. A neuter or spay can also make a nice "auntie," but unless you know from experience that they are absolutely trustworthy, don't allow them access to the litter when you're not there to watch. Sometimes kittens will even suckle an agreeable foster parent even though it has no milk.

Most queens are quite benign towards the presence of other cats as long as the babies are in the nest. But once the babies are up and running around, she'll become very protective and irascible, ready to trounce innocent bystanders at the first squeal from her kittens.

If you have several litters of different sizes together, be sure that the smaller kittens are not being neglected. Queens will usually try to steal the largest kittens from other nests, thinking perhaps that bigger means better. You may find both queens together in one nest nursing the older babies, while the younger ones are going hungry. If this is happening, you'll have to separate the litters.

Elimination

The newborn kitten is unable to eliminate its wastes unless it is stimulated. The queen does this by licking the kitten's bottom and lapping up the waste. The urine should be clear; the feces a pale to dark gold in color and of the consistency of toothpaste.

However, the *first* feces – the meconium – will be black and sticky, perhaps in small balls or pellets. The meconium forms in the intestines of the fetus. It will be expelled within twenty-four hours after birth. You will often not see it at all.

A new mother may fail to stimulate her kittens sufficiently, resulting in a build-up of toxic wastes that can cause death in the newborn in less than a day. Therefore, you should insure correct elimination by stimulating each kitten twice a day. You can also encourage the queen to do her job by raising the kitten's tail and holding it, bottom up, to her face. Usually she gets the idea within a day or two, and then you no longer need to be concerned.

Take a few balls of cotton and dampen them slightly with warm water. Then, holding the kitten on its back, dab gently at its bottom a few times. If your efforts are usually rewarded, you may assume that the mother is not yet doing her job and you should continue helping.

If a kitten has mild diarrhea and fouls itself, you can wash it in some warm water and place it back in the nest. Newborns dry quickly and a bath will do no harm to a healthy kitten. Once the kitten has grown some coat, however, you must dry it thoroughly yourself, as the long hair will retain the moisture and the kitten will be chilled. Dry the kitten in a hot towel by massaging all over, or use a blow-dryer set on low.

Parasites in the nest

The newborn cannot protect itself from parasites, so you must do it for him. By far the best course is to free the environment of fleas *before* the kittens are born. Flea sprays and powders should not be used on the kittens or their mother. In the very young kitten you'll see the fleas because the hair is still sparse; in older kittens look for "flea dirt" above the base of the tail – little bits of flea excrement in the fur.

Fleas can be removed manually by dabbing them with a cotton swab dipped in alcohol. This stuns them for a few seconds, so if you're quick you can tweeze them off. Don't attempt to crush them. They're built in a flattened shape anyway (as an aid in moving through forests of hair). Dip the tweezers in a cup of water mixed with alcohol and they'll soon drown.

Changing the bedding daily will help, too. In the case of a really bad infestation, rub a bit of sevin dust (5% Sevin, available in gardening supply stores) under the kitten's chin and along its backbone. Rub and blow out as much excess as you can. What remains will help keep the fleas down. The mother will probably not need treating, since any fleas on her will have transferred to the kittens; they recognize the more vulnerable host.

After the kittens are about six weeks of age, they can safely be dipped or bathed to remove fleas. You must use an insecticidal shampoo or dip, because bathing alone will not kill fleas. It might be best to use the products at half strength for safety's sake.

If there are flies around, do your utmost to keep them away from the newborn kitten or it may become flyblown. The sick or wounded animal should also be kept away from fly-infested areas for the same reason.

Sexing the kittens

A few people can't tell the sex of adult cats, much less tiny kittens. The classic formula is that the male kitten's anus and genital opening look like a colon (:), and the female's like a semicolon (;). In addition, the male's openings are farther apart than the female's. The kittens with broader heads and wider shoulders are usually males, though my all-time biggest kitten was a female.

Until you've raised several litters you will look for punctuation marks in vain on the tiny creatures, which are sure to be squirming and screaming throughout. Compare the kittens with each other, and assuming both sexes are represented, you'll soon get the idea. If you're not certain, have your vet sex the kittens when you take them for their first shots. Kitten buyers always take the breeder's word as to sex, and you don't want to be embarrassed by someone calling later on to say that the female kitten you sold him has grown up into a big, solid tom!

The kitten's eyes

The newborn's eyes are normally closed at birth and open five to ten days thereafter. The opening will first appear as a dark slit at the inside corner of the eye. This will gradually enlarge until, within twenty-four hours or so, the eye is completely opened. All kittens in the litter should open their eyes at approximately the same time.

If the eyes have still not opened at fourteen days, massage the eyelid gently with warm water and then, grasping the hair on the upper and lower lids, *gently* attempt to pull the lids apart at the inside corner. Make just a tiny opening, then allow the eyes to open the rest of the way naturally. The lids will usually come apart quite easily at this age.

The new eyes are invariably a milky blue-gray: the color fills in later. The eyes are very sensitive to light for the first few days, so the kittens should not be exposed to bright lights. This is true, in fact, even *before* the eyes begin to open, since light does penetrate the lids.

When I notice the eyes just beginning to open, I trim all the kittens' front claws. This is a delicate job but well worth the effort, since it prevents injury to the eyeball when the kittens are nursing. Remember to get just the very tips of the claws. This will also prevent scratching and subsequent infection of the queen's nipples as the kittens become more vigorous.

Occasionally a kitten will be born with its eyes open. This is quite common in some of the short-hair breeds. There should be no problem with this if the blinking mechanism is working (that is, if the kitten is able to close its eyes). However, if the kitten does not seem to be able to blink or close its eyes, the eyeball can dry out. Keep the eyeball moistened with a few drops of saline solution (use the sterile solution made for contact lens wearers) every couple of hours, or as often as possible. If you must be away longer, or at night, coat the eyeball with a thin film of antibiotic ointment. Call your vet for advice.

Once the kitten's eyes have opened normally, check them twice a day. Mild infection seems to set in quite easily, so look for any sign of guminess or pus. If the lids are gummed together, massage them gently with warm water or baby oil on a cotton ball, then pull the lids gently apart. Flush out any pus with saline solution, and finish with a film of antibiotic ointment. Make sure you are using a mild *opthalmic* ointment. You'll find that the eyes gradually improve and within a week or so are bright and clear. Continue using the ointment as long as any signs of guminess or pus are present.

The ear canals, closed at birth, open a few days after the eyes.

The two-week old kittens

At around two weeks of age the kittens will start exploring their world; first the nest, then the big world outside. These explorations coincide with the kitten's ability to support its weight on the legs instead of the belly. Learning to walk doesn't happen all at once, of course, and the kittens will totter and fall over regularly.

Between two the three weeks you'll also notice the kitten's first efforts at grooming themselves and at playing.

By now the kittens are real pros at nursing — not just hanging onto a nipple, but also the techniques for landing the biggest, fattest, milkiest nipple of them all. One favorite method is crawling up over the mother's back and sliding down onto the heads of the other kittens, thus dislodging them, and grabbing a nipple before they can sort themselves out.

Litter-box training starts when the kittens first leave their nest. The instinct to dig and eliminate in dirt is as instinctive as walking, and all you need to do is provide a litter box near the nest. For the first few days, the top of a cardboard shoe box works well, as they are easily able to climb into it. Don't be disturbed if the kittens start out by eating the litter; they'll soon get the right idea. You can help by placing all the kittens in the box right after each meal. Be sure to keep the litter scrupulously clean. That's all there is to "box-training." Be prepared for an occasional slip-up, however, when the kittens are playing far from their box. You might put a box into each room for a few weeks while the babies are learning control.

Socializing the kittens

Right from the moment of birth you should be gently handling the kittens twice a day. This will happen automatically if you're elimination-testing or supplementing their feeding. Studies have shown that kittens given this hand-ling early in life become better socialized with humans than those that don't; additionally, health and vigor are promoted by mild stress. Young kittens soon overcome their fear and will sniff and explore your hand, innately curious even before their eyes have opened.

After they're about three weeks old, encourage visitors to handle the kittens, too, but don't allow anyone, ever, to chase the kittens or frighten them. Far from being anxious at the presence of strangers, most queens are obviously pleased to be admired and will give a special demonstration of what good mothers they are for the benefit of visitors.

The kittens should have the run of the house by the time they're about five weeks old, if not sooner, to accustom them to various types of flooring and furniture. If they can safely become acquainted with other animals during this time, so much the better.

You must do all in your power to develop outgoing, fearless kittens. Those first several weeks will have an effect on the kittens that will last their lifetimes.

Weaning the kittens

Kitten Milk Replacement (KMR) is available at most pet shops. You can make your own formula, an approximation of cat's milk, as follows: one can of evaporated milk, one can of evaporated skimmed milk, two egg yolks, and liquid vitamins. Optional: a spoonful a plain yogurt. This formula can be stored for about a week. It's cheaper and probably fresher than KMR.

The formula can be offered to the pregnant queen daily for about two weeks before kittening and during nursing. It can be used to supplement the natural mother's milk or to raise orphan kittens, and again for weaning. Evaporated goat's milk, if available, can be substituted in the formula for the cow's milk. I've not found any advantage in doing so, but goat's milk is supposed to be more easily digestible.

Most people wean their kittens at about five weeks. My purpose in offering formula to the kittens at three weeks is not to wean the kittens away from their mother at that time, but to supplement the mother's milk, which may not be enough to support a big litter, and to give the smaller kittens a chance to boost their milk intake.

If the kittens are not interested, I try again the next day. By four weeks of age all the kittens are lapping from a saucer. The reluctant ones can be encouraged by holding them up to the saucer so they can't back away and dipping their noses into the formula. Offer the formula twice a day.

In the meantime, the kittens are still nursing from the queen. Very gradually, they begin taking less milk from their mother and more from the saucer until by about six weeks they rarely nurse from the queen. At this age, which might be called "the age of sharp teeth," the queen will be reluctant to let the kittens nurse. A third meal of formula daily should be offered as soon as it's apparent that the kittens are not nursing from the queen.

At about four and a half to five weeks of age, the transition from formula to solid food can begin. Place a small dab of any strained-meat baby food in the center of the saucer. The kittens will get to it as they lap up the milk. Gradually increase the amount of baby food mixed into the formula, putting it in small dabs over the saucer and pouring the warmed formula over it. By six weeks of age, all the kittens will be eating the baby food/formula mixture. This is by far the easiest method for weaning kittens I've found. The process is very gradual and free of stress for the kittens; it is not necessary to starve them to force them to eat the meat. If baby food is offered separately from the formula, the kittens naturally prefer the formula and ignore the meat.

A final transition can be made from baby food to your regular menu using the same technique, gradually mixing the two together until the baby food is eliminated. By the time your kittens are ready for their new homes (ten to twelve weeks of age), they will be completely weaned and eating a regular diet, although they should continue getting three meals a day until they are four to six months old.

The final stage in preparing a cat for his adult diet is getting him to accept dried food. Dry food is a necessary supplement to every cat's meals and a bowl can be left out for nibbling through the day. But most kittens don't like dry food, possibly because it hurts their gums during their second teething (the permanent teeth, at about five months). A little dry food can be mixed into the food at mealtimes and thus accustom the cat to this last, essential part of his diet.

Variety is especially important while kittens are growing up. The kitten raised on a single food is likely to never accept anything else. See the section on feeding for a list of products to offer your kittens.

Vaccinating kittens

There is so much variation in vaccination programs recommended for young kittens that the best course is to ask your vet and follow his advice, whether you are vaccinating the kittens yourself or taking them to him. The reason for this variation is that it's impossible to known exactly when the young kitten's immunity gives out. The kittens ingest antibodies with their mother's milk that protect them as long as they're nursing (this is why orphan kittens that are bottle or tube-fed will need vaccinations sooner than naturally-raised kittens). At some point between five and twelve weeks of age, the level of antibodies in the kitten's bloodstream deteriorates; the kitten then requires vaccination in order to build its own immunity system. Until this level of maternal immunity wears off, any vaccinations given will be wasted because the antibodies will fight off the vaccine. But because there's no way of telling when the level decreases (and it can be different in each kitten), one gambles with the kitten's health by waiting too long to give the first shots.

The age at which the maternal antibodies are nearly certain to be absent is twelve weeks; therefore, one set of vaccinations should always be given at this time. The question is when to give the earlier shots. Some recommend nine and twelve weeks, others, six, nine and twelve weeks, still others, seven, ten and thirteen weeks.

Vaccinations will include those for feline enteritis, rhinotracheitis, calicivirus and possibly pneumonitis. A shot against rabies should be unecessary unless the kitten is going to be air shipped, cross an international border, or have access to areas where it may be bitten by dogs, stray cats or wild animals.

Record all vaccines given to your kittens and cats, whether given by yourself or a vet. Include the date, type, maker and serial number of the vaccine. This information should be kept in your permanent record and also given to the person who purchases the kitten. Such records will be needed if problems arise.

There are two basic types of vaccines: killed and modified live. The former gives a passive immunity; the latter builds up the kitten's own immunity. The modified live vaccines are preferred by many vets as they tend to give a higher-level, longer-lasting immunity. Some breeders have had problems with them, however. If in doubt, talk to other breeders in your order to find out what they use. You'll find that a few breeders feel the vaccines are a greater health risk to their kittens than giving no vaccines at all. Do not follow their example. The kittens you sell as pets will be going into a variety of new environments over which you have no control. Complete vaccinations are essential.

Giving your own vaccinations

Most experienced cat breeders give their own vaccinations. By doing so they not only save money and time, but avoid the risk of infection inherent in leaving the home environment. There are three types of injections: subcutaneous ("under the skin"), intramuscular, and intravenous. Everyone can learn to give subcutaneous injections, which are simple and safe.

Vaccines are available, in order of preference, from your vet and from veterinary supply houses. Although the vet supply houses serve vets as well as breeders, vets will be up-to-date on the best types of vaccines to use at any particular time. A vet who has already vaccinated several litters of kittens for a customer might not object to selling her the vaccines along with instructions in their use.

Since some veterinarians are reluctant to demonstrate subcutaneous injections and to sell vaccines, a experienced breeder should be your second choice. She can give you the address of a veterinary supply house.

Vaccines can be safely stored in your refrigerator and brought to room temperature just before use. The vaccines are always shipped by air in insulated containers, since heat will cause them to deteriorate. They should be kept sealed against light. Note the expiration date on the label.

The vaccines come in either a liquid form or a powder form that must be mixed with a diluent. In the latter case, you'll receive two tiny vials for each injection; they will be mixed immediately before use. The liquid vaccines may also come in individual or multi-dose vials; the latter are usually cheaper. Other vaccines come in a pre-measured dose in a syringe.

Disposable syringes and needles are either included with the vaccines or purchased separately. You must *never* try to save the small amount they cost by reusing a disposable syringe. Each syringe and needle comes sealed in a plastic container that should not be removed until ready to use. Anyone having syringes and needles in the house should store them safely, locked away from children and well out of sight of visitors. After use, the syringes should be disposed of with equal care. Breeders' access to syringes, needles, vaccines and other medications can be withdrawn by law if too many abuse their right to purchase them, or hand out the names and addresses of vet supply houses indiscriminately. Some vet supply houses require that you be recommended by one of their clients when you order for the first time, and it is always best to give them such recommendations and your cattery registration name and number when writing them for the first time.

To give a subcutaneous injection, first prepare the vaccine. Attach the needle to the syringe tip. A few screw on, but most are just a friction-fit. Draw air into the syringe to about the 3cc mark. Insert the needle into the diluent or the vaccine and depress the plunger to force air into the vial. Now turn the vial over, withdraw the needle almost to the rubber stopper, and pull out the plunger to draw the liquid into the syringe.

If the vaccine is a powder, you must now insert the diluent into the vial of powder, then withdraw the needle and shake the mixture for a few seconds. Now withdraw the liquid from the vial into the syringe. Depress the plunger to express a drop of vaccine before inserting it into the skin. Keep the needle upright to keep the liquid in the bottom of the syringe. Try to avoid injecting an air bubble under the skin (if you do get a little air under the skin, it will gradually disperse and do not harm; it is only in intravenous injections that an air bubble can be fatal).

You need not change the needle between withdrawing the liquid from the vial and vaccinating the kitten, but do use a different needle for each kitten.

A subcutaneous injection can be given virtually anywhere on the body where the skin is fairly loose. In cats, it is given in the scruff of the neck. A loose fold of skin is lifted and the needle inserted into the base. Afterwards, the spot should be massaged for a few minutes to dissipate the vaccine under the skin. The entire process takes only a minute. Difficulties are rare, and usually are due to a lack of cleanliness that results in an infection at the site of the puncture.

Subcutaneous fluids such as Ringer's, used to combat dehydration, can be injected twice a day into the kitten or cat. Start with about 6cc for a kitten, 10cc for a cat, and increase the amount next time if the fluids are absorbed immediately. These amounts are too large to disperse under the skin of the neck, and should be given under the skin of the ribcage, holding the needle at a very shallow angle (almost parallel to the body).

The exact method of giving subcutaneous injections should preferably be demonstrated to the novice by her veterinarian or by an experienced breeder. Some breeders are never able to overcome their squeamishness. If you are at all reluctant, you should continue to have your kittens vaccinated by your vet. If you have many kittens and cats, you should be able to get a volume discount, and you could also try to find a vet that will come to your house.

Caring for orphans

Besides feeding and evacuating the kittens as already described, the breeder will have to provide additional warmth for orphans. Sometimes a neutered cat or even a small dog can be a substitute for the queen's warmth, if it will agree to nest with the kittens. Failing that, you will have to provide artificial heat. Optimum temperature in the nest should be around ninety degrees for the first three days, eighty-five degrees for the following week, and eighty degrees for the week after that. The kitten's internal temperature control will have stabilized by then, and it will need only moderate temperatures after the third week. Heat can be provided by a heating pad, space heater, egg incubator, or other method. Keep a thermometer in the nest to check the heat. If the kittens start to sleep apart from each other rather than the normal pile-up, lower the heat a little.

Some authorities recommend that orphans be raised in separate compartments because of the possibility of having ears, tails and genitals damaged by littermates' suckling them. However, if the orphans are fed adequately and often, they will be better off together. If the orphans are separated they should be brought together at about three weeks or as soon as they leave the nest.

Orphans should be massaged all over with a damp cotton ball or soft cloth to simulate maternal care, at least once a day. Special attention should be given to the eyes, which seem to need this stimulus to open naturally.

Your vet should be notified at once if you have an orphan litter. Those kittens that fail to receive the colostrum, the first maternal milk that is especially rich in antibodies, will need a special program of immunization. You should also contact friends who are experienced breeders for their advice, and maybe even a substitute mother.

Every cat breeder should be prepared to raise an orphan litter, for almost every breeder will at some point have to do so. If you have the equipment already on hand, and if you're already familiar with bottle-feeding and tube-feeding techniques, you will not be so alarmed when faced with a litter or orphans.

Supplemental feeding and feeding orphans

As long as the kittens are gaining weight steadily and are not crying, they are getting sufficient milk from their mother and do not require supplemental feeding. If one or two seems to be getting the worse of the competition for nipples and begins losing weight, supplemental feeding should be given. If the queen has died, has no milk, or is unwilling to stay with her babies, the litter will have to be fed on a regular schedule.

The only difference between supplemental feeding and feeding orphans is in frequency of feeding.

There are four methods for getting formulae from the bottle to the stomach: eye dropper, syringe, nursing bottle, and tube feeding.

When feeding with an eye dropper, the idea is to draw formula into the dropper, hold it to the kitten's mouth and allow the milk to flow slowly into the mouth. The danger with this method is that it's too tempting to force the milk into the mouth; if the kitten can't swallow quickly enough, it will inhale milk into its lungs and die later of pneumonia. The only recommendation for using an eye dropper is that most people have one at hand.

A syringe can be used in the same way as the eye dropper but has the same drawbacks. Its only advantages over the eye-dropper is that one can see exactly the amount of formula being taken, and that the tip of the syringe is usually smaller and can be more easily inserted into the side of the kitten's mouth.

Feeding Chart for Orphans

Age (days)	Weight	cc's per feeding	teaspoons per feeding	hrs between feedings
Birth	3 oz	3cc	½t	3
3	4	4cc	¾t	3
6	5	5cc	⅞t	3
8	6	6cc	1t	3
10	7	8cc	1½t	4
14	8	12cc	2t	4
18	10	15cc	2½t	4
24	12	18cc	3t	5

At 24 to 28 days age, the kittens should learn to take formula from a saucer. They should receive four feedings daily of all they can eat.

A special small-animal feeding bottle can be obtained from your vet, from a pet shop, or from a vet supply house, but the one commonly on the market (made by Borden) is useless for newborn kittens. The nipple is too large and much too stiff. Harder to find but worth the effort is the Catac bottle and nipple. Doll bottles will also work in a pinch, better than the Borden bottle. The size of the nipple and the hole in the nipple is important; too small and the kitten will not be able to withdraw enough milk, too large and the milk will flow too quickly into the kitten's mouth, making it choke and splutter.

Lacking tube feeding equipment or a proper bottle, a sponge can be used in an emergency. Cut a small "nipple" with a larger piece attached (you must be sure the kitten cannot swallow the sponge itself) and soak it with warm formula. Insert into the kitten's mouth and allow it to nurse for a minute; repeat as necessary.

In all the above methods, the willingness and ability of the kitten to nurse must be taken into account. With the eye-dropper and syringe, the tip is inserted into the side of the mouth. The kitten can either nurse from it (which it will seldom do) or the milk can be forced into the mouth very gradually; the presence of liquid in the mouth stimulating the swallowing reflex — hopefully. The bottle has a more natural nipple and the kitten may nurse willingly. A sick or passive kitten, however, will not be willing or able to nurse at all, or even to swallow. For this reason, and several others, most breeders consider tube-feeding the method of choice.

Tube feeding equipment consists of a flexible rubber tube that can be attached to a syringe. The end of the tube is pushed gently past the throat until it reaches the stomach, and formula forced into the stomach by depressing the syringe. The danger of the kitten inhaling liquid is nil, since the tube bypasses the windpipe. Tube feeding allows precise amounts to be fed whether or not the kitten is able to nurse. And it is a great time-saver: a bottle-fed kitten will nurse for fifteen to forty-five minutes at a time, making the feeding of an entire litter a round-the-clock task and the feeding of several litters an impossibility. An entire litter of kittens can be tube-fed in about five minutes.

If you want to try tube feeding, buy the right equipment. *You cannot manufacture your own.* The proper tubes are sturdy, flexible, have an enlarged end that friction-fits onto a syringe and a rounded tip to prevent injury to the stomach. The liquid comes out two holes at the sides of the tip. The tubes come in several sizes. Buy the smallest (the mini-tube) and the next size up. They're quite cheap and do wear out rapidly, so buy several at a time. Many vet supply houses sell them, or you might be able to borrow some from a friend.

The danger of inserting the tube into the lungs by mistake is practically non-existent. In several years of tube feeding, I have never inserted a tube into a kitten's lungs.

The best way to learn to tube feed is to ask an experienced breeder or vet to demonstrate the technique. However, lacking such a demonstration, proceed as follows. First, mark the tube at the proper length for insertion into the stomach. Hold the tip of the tube alongside the kitten's mouth and bend it alongside the kitten's neck and along the ribcage to the last rib. Mark around the tube at this spot with a bit of tape, a marker pen, nail polish, or anything else that will stick to the rubber. If you have kittens of different sizes, measure for the smallest kitten. The mark is only approximate anyway. If you don't get the tube completely into the stomach, it will just flow down into the esophagus – another tube – and then into the stomach. You'll need to replace the mark weekly as the kitten grows.

Now fill the syringe with warmed formula, either through the tube or through the syringe tip. Friction-fit the tube onto the tip of the syringe quite firmly, as you don't want it to pop off (this won't do any harm – just make a mess). Depress the plunger until formula comes out the end of the tube. Dip the entire end of the tube into the formula.

Hold the kitten upright in one hand and aim the tube into the mouth towards the back of the throat with the other. It will bend around the back of the mouth and thread quite easily down the throat. If it doesn't go down easily, withdraw it slightly and try again. Keep "threading" until you are close to the mark on the tube. If the kitten is screaming, you'll know you're in the right spot – it couldn't possibly scream with a tube in its lungs! Now hold the tube in place by closing your hand around both the tube and the kitten's head. If the kitten is struggling the tube can be withdrawn without your being aware of it, so be sure the tube stays exactly in place until you're finished. Depress the syringe slowly to force the formula into the stomach. Count out five to ten seconds as you do so, to avoid inflating the stomach too rapidly. Then withdraw the tube. Wash both tube and syringe with lukewarm water, followed by cold sterilizer, and leave them to soak in the sterilizer. Clean inside the tube by pressing or drawing water, then the sterilizer, through it with the syringe. Be sure to rinse the sterilizer solution off before using it again.

After several uses the tubes become too limp, which makes them bend sideways in the kitten's mouth rather than threading down the throat. The plastic syringes will also wear out, so buy several. The cold sterilizer is not essential; thorough rinsing with warm water will suffice. Cleanliness, not absolute sterility, is the goal. Remember that a mother's nipples are far from sterile! Do not use hot water to wash the tubes as it will make the tubes lose their stiffness.

Tube feeding can also be used to feed the anorexic older kitten. The main difficulty is the kitten's teeth. Once the tube is inserted, clamp the jaws shut over the tube to hold it in place and prevent the teeth from shearing off the tube. If the formula does not go in easily, release your hold a little, as you are clamping the tube shut as well as the jaws. The tubes are actually quite sturdy and not easily punctured. I have successfully force fed four- and five-month old kittens with tube feeding equipment. It is certainly preferable to the messy technique of squashing food into the mouth and convincing the kitten to swallow it.

Tube feeding is not a miracle-cure and is not risk-free, but it is an essential technique for the breeder's repertoire. Remember to use the proper formula and never try to substitute cow's milk. In the case of an older kitten being force fed, strained baby food, baby cereal, egg yolks, etc., can be liquified and added to the KMR or formula.

Amounts to feed

For the first five days, newborns should be fed every three hours, 1cc of formula per ounce of weight (weight is two and a half to three ounces in most newborns). If you are tube feeding, use the small syringe that is marked in cc's to determine the amount. The accompanying chart gives both cc's and table-spoon measurements for feeding.

After the first week, until they reach the age of two and a half weeks, the kittens can be fed every four hours. At that age, every effort should be made to teach them to lap from a saucer. Continue feeding by other methods as long as it takes them to learn, feeding every six hours. All kittens should be lapping milk from a saucer by three and a half weeks, if not sooner. For those who merely wish to supplement the milk received from the queen, the same amounts can be fed two or three times a day.

After each feeding, orphan kittens should have their bowels evacuated by the method already described.

Kitten mortalities

About 40% of all kitten mortalities during the first week are attributed by breeders to the "fading kitten" syndrome. Such kittens appear quite normal and nurse vigorously for a day or two. Then you'll notice one that is no longer nursing; it may cry feebly or become silent and withdrawn; its movements are undirected and it will lie stretched out, away from the others. Within about twenty-four hours it dies. Sometimes one kitten after another in the same litter will succumb.

Some kittens are born malnourished because of poor nutrition in the dam. These kittens may be too weak to nurse effectively; consequently they receive inadequate milk from the queen which makes them even weaker, a cycle that terminates in death.

If your cattery has had a recent problem with "fading kitten," it might be wise to start supplemental feeding for all kittens within a few hours after birth. Keep an accurate record of weight gain, if you're not already doing so. A growth and weight chart for a typical litter is given on page 88.

Bacterial infections also cause many kitten deaths. Hypothermia, insufficient nourishment and dehydration can be observed in a wrinkled skin, poor muscle tone, and cool feel to the body, compared to the normal kitten (see the section on the ailing kitten).

The sick kitten can be placed in an incubator or on a heating pad adjusted to 85 degrees. Stimulate circulation with gentle massage and turning. If the queen can hear or smell the kitten she will become anxious, so keep the sick one well away from the rest of the litter. The severely dehydrated kitten can be tube-fed a 5% to 15% glucose solution obtained from your vet, 1 to 2 cc's every half hour. Formula should not be fed until the kitten's condition has improved.

In some cases, antibiotics and gamma globulin serum can be effective; these can be administered by your vet. In practice, it's almost impossible to diagnose the source of illness in a newborn kitten. Providing proper care and the administration of fluids will enable some to recover; others will die no matter what you do. An occasional death should be regarded as unavoidable. A high kitten mortality rate, however, must be seriously investigated.

A necropsy is rarely useful on a very small kitten; however, you should consider one for all kittens that die after four or five weeks of age (consult your vet). These may reveal genetic defects in your bloodlines or sources of infection in your cattery. If a dead kitten cannot be necropsied at once, store its body in the refrigerator – not the freezer – and take it to your vet as soon as possible. The longer the tissues deteriorate, the less they will reveal.

Preventing a high kitten mortality rate can be accomplished by selecting sound breeding stock and keeping the health of all animals optimal, by providing the queen with good nourishment, and by providing the kittens with a clean environment, adequate heat, attention to weight gain and quick veterinary assistance when problems are suspected.

Litter registration

Once your kittens are three or four weeks old, you will want to register the litter. You can send in the registration as soon as they're born, but you may lose some or all the litter during the high-risk period of the first week, so it's better to wait until you know you'll have some live kittens. In some cases, you may not be sure of the colors of your kittens until they are older.

The one registering association that is universally accepted by all associations, including overseas, is CFA. Therefore, to be certain that the kittens you sell can be registered and shown anywhere, you must register the litter with CFA. CFA will not register any cats, except imports, that have not been litter-registered first. Even if you never intend to show a cat in a CFA show, you should litter-register with CFA for the sake of your kitten buyers. You should also litter-register your kittens in the other associations in which you show your cats, if they require it. Or you can litter-register CFA and individually register in any other associations in which you show. The fees are small.

Write to CFA and any other associations for their litter registration form. The form will have spaces to list the dam, sire, and each kitten in the litter. If outside stud service was used, the stud's owner will have to sign the litter registration before you send it in. You can also register kittens individually at the same time you send in the litter registration. Normally you'll do this only for kittens you intend to keep.

If you have any kittens in the litter that you are thinking of keeping and showing, check your calendar for upcoming shows for which that kitten will be eligible (when it is between four and eight months of age). Most breeders will adjust the date of birth by a day or two if it will enable them to enter a kitten that would otherwise be just a bit too young. Other breeders condemn this common practice as unethical. However, if you consider that the *true* age of a kitten is dated from its moment of conception, and that gestation varies in each cat, you'll see that a kitten born on May 1 after sixty days' gestation is actually *younger* than a kitten born on May 5 after seventy days' gestation.

There is, however, another practice in which the date of birth is changed by weeks and even months so that a kitten being shown is really much older than the other kittens competing. This practice arises because, all other things being equal, a more mature kitten has an advantage over its rivals. This uncommon practice *is* unethical. Its intent is to deceive and gain an unfair advantage over the competition. Judges who suspect this practice can check a kitten's teeth. A "four month old" kitten with a full set of adult teeth is highly questionable.

Once you've sent in your litter registration, CFA will return to you a certificate of registration for the litter as well as a blue slip for each kitten in the litter. This blue slip will be signed by you and turned over to the kitten buyer, who will send it in for individual registration of the kitten. In the case of kittens sold as pets with an alteration agreement, the blue slip has a box at the bottom to check to indicate that the kitten cannot be used for breeding, and a line for the buyer's signature to insure that he agrees to this provision. Or you can withhold the blue slip until the purchaser has furnished proof of altering (a note from the vet performing the operation).

When a kitten is bought for breeding or showing, the blue slip should be given to the purchaser when the kitten is sold, or, if a check is written, sent to the purchaser after the check has cleared. Once the purchaser has the kitten's blue slip, he can register the kitten as his own and the breeder's options in case of non-payment or non-fulfillment of agreements are lessened. Without the registration papers, the new owner cannot show or register litters from the cat. However, he is still legally the owner – courts of law recognize proof of sale (a receipt of payment or cancelled check), and not registration papers, in determining ownership.

The major associations

There are nine major cat associations, of which CFA is the largest. Some of the others tend to be localized, so that if you move from one part of the country to another you will be attending shows of another association. In general, CFA, ACFA and TICA shows are held nationwide. These are the three largest associations. Breed standards are fairly constant from one association to the next, though breed names may differ, especially for the newer breeds. Show regulations are similar from one association to the next. Presumably the judges in one association will look for something a bit different from those in another, so that you'll hear of a particular cat that "he's a CFA cat," or "he won't do well in TICA."

When choosing a breed, make sure it is recognized for showing by every association in your area. Cats in *provisional* breeds or new color varieties of a traditional breed can be shown, but not for championship status. Their division is called *AOV*: All Other Varieties, or a similar name depending on association, and there are usually no more than a handful at any show.

Joining associations and clubs

You can register a cattery name, kittens and cats with an association and show your cats under that association without being an actual member. In some cases you need not even register the cat you intend to show, though you will have to register it after the show if you want to have its wins recognized towards a championship or towards regional and national honors.

Local cat clubs are formed within each assocation. The cat clubs pay fees to the association and hold shows under its rules. Cat clubs may hold regular meetings with guest speakers, they may organize health and genetic seminars, but their primary task will be putting on one or more shows annually. Almost anyone can form a cat club and hold shows, but previous experience is essential. Such experience can be gained by joining a local cat club *or* volunteering to help in setting up a show. Many clubs are rather insular, and the novice should not expect an invitation to join. All, however, welcome volunteer help at shows, so this is an excellent way for a beginner to learn about showing and perhaps be invited to join a club.

Many cat shows are break-even events; some make money and a few lose money. Many shows donate their profits to research organizations. Despite entry fees of, currently, $20 to $35 per cat for a four-ring, one-day show, plus a gate receipt from spectators, a cat show has high expenses: show-hall rental, judges' fees, lodging and transportation, cage purchase or rental, catalog preparation and printing, advertising and publicity.

Many people show their cats for years without ever joining a cat club, but a club can be a valuable source of contacts and information for the novice, as well as a fascinating view at the inside workings of cat shows. Most clubs hold monthly meetings.

Shows as an evaluation of a breeding program

Cat shows give the breeder an objective evaluation of his breeding program's success and a chance to study those cats that the judges feel are of highest merit — for only when we can clearly *see* where one cat differs from another can we hope to effectively select the best cats for our own breeding programs.

Yet, in one sense, cat shows fail to point the way for breeders. At cat shows, importance is given to the individual, without reference to its antecedants or its progeny. A cat of outstanding appearance will occasionally be produced from bloodlines otherwise lacking in distinction. The converse holds true: some of the great sires of every species and breed were themselves poor specimens that could never set foot inside a show ring.

In some types of animal exhibitions, special breeding classes are held in which a sire or dam and several progeny are judged as a whole. Such classes were formerly held at cat shows, but are never seen today, perhaps due to the expense involved in entering more than one or two cats.

Politics

You'll go to many shows before you begin to recognize all the judges and their preferences, but you'll probably hear something about "politics" at the very first one. A win, or failure to win, is said to be politically motivated if the judge makes an award to a friend, or in return for a favor. Of course it happens — it happens in every form of competition that is based on judgment rather than performance. But the majority of judges are fair and conscientious.

Why does it happen so often, then, that the placings within each class are different from one judge to the next? Standards admit a variety of interpretation, and judges may prefer certain types within a breed. The cats being shown are often extremely close in merit. They may each have different flaws, and a judge may consider one flaw more serious than another, depending partly on his own experience breeding cats.

A truly superior kitten or cat will win wherever and to whomever it is shown, regardless of whether the exhibitor is a newcomer or an old hand.

The purpose of showing

Shows are an exhibition of skill. They are also, of course, a sort of beauty pageant for cats, but their primary purpose should be a test of the breeder's skill. The purebred cat is a creation of its breeder, and it is mainly to the breeder that credit should go for a win.

In practice, people show for a variety of reasons. There's nothing quite like winning ribbons, and at cat shows the ribbons fly thick and fast, much to the bewilderment of casual onlookers. Unlike the dog show and horse show worlds, where only a few take home anything but debts, it's the rare cat owner who goes home empty-handed. Championships become meaningless in the less-popular breeds, since they can be earned by default. The big guys go after the finals, regional and national awards. But even the little guy eventually ends up with a wall full of ribbons.

Cat breeders whose friends are also in cats have a lot of fun fraternizing at shows. Novices can especially benefit by introducing themselves to the more experienced breeders there. Even the shy can get ideas on grooming and presentation by watching the experts.

Accustoming your cat to showing

The cat destined for a show career should be shown as a kitten to accustom it to the strange sights and sounds and handling by the judge, even though it will not earn points towards its championship. Kittens can be shown without registration numbers, but an adult cat cannot.

Mature toms that are accustomed to being shown should not present a problem. During breeding season, however, many toms become difficult to handle. If your tom is feeling ornery and you fear he may attempt to bite or scratch the judge, by all means mention this to the judge's clerk when you bring him to the judging ring. The judge will probably ask you to take the tom from his cage yourself before he handles it. You should not be embarrassed by this; it is far better than having the judge scratched or bitten by your tom. At a show, you might notice that the cats' numbers are not always placed sequentially on the cages in the judging rings, or there may be empty cages between cats. This is to separate toms so that they are not in adjoining cages.

The queen is less likely to demonstrate her annoyance than is the tom; nevertheless, the same strictures apply.

A nursing queen, of couse, will not be shown because of the danger of carrying home some infection to her litter — the youngsters being more susceptible than a mature cat — as well as the inadvisability of separating her from her litter for so long. Pregnant queens or those recently mated and thought to be pregnant are sometimes shown up through their fourth week of pregnancy.

What about the queen in heat? Alas, entries must be made weeks in advance of the show and it is futile to attempt to predict heat periods. Rather than throw away the money, you could show a queen you thought to be just entering her heat period. Quite often the strange situation will cause a queen to go off her heat for a day or two. This is fine at the shows, but not so nice when we bundle her off to be bred and she clouts the eager grand champion right across the nose.

The cost of showing

Showing can be either a huge expense or no expense at all. You do not really *have* to show in order to sell your kittens. But your show entry fee does more than give you a chance at ribbons: it gives you an estimate of your cat's worth, introduces you to other breeders, gives you possible access to their stud cats, helps you make contacts for future kitten sales, allows you to pick up a wealth of information, and promotes purebred cats.

The current entry fee is about $28 to $50 for one cat, one show (one or two days). Add to this the extras such as a double-sized cage, special grooming equipment, not to mention gas and hotel charges, and you can tote up $150 or so without half trying. To campaign a cat for regional honors can come to $3000 or more, and to campaign a cat nation-wide — well, I hate to think about that one, but if you ever have a cat that good, you should certainly give it a try. Campaigners fly from one show to another almost every weekend of the year. They often enter two or three shows for each weekend and then go to the show with the best count (number of cats entered), since their ultimate total depends on how many cats they have defeated. A show weekend including airfare will average around $550, so you can see just how much money – and time – it takes. Campaigning a kitten is a little different, since kittens are kittens for only four months. The end-of-season total for a kitten will depend not merely on its quality, but when it was born. A "mid-summer" kitten will find fewer shows and much smaller kitten entries than later in the year.

Assuming that you are not yet ready to spend $30,000 campaigning your cat, do at least attend all the local shows in the association of your choice.

Promoting at the shows

Cat shows offer an excellent opportunity to promote your cats. Shows attract spectators; often these are cat lovers who are choosing a breed to purchase as a pet. You need not slink away from contact with spectators if your cat fails to win. Spectators are usually so confused by the judging system and the plethora of ribbons that they couldn't for the life of them tell which cat won what ("how can they *all* be the best Siamese?"). Those looking for a pet are searching for a cat they like, not necessarily the one the judges like best.

Your cat is on display to these people at all times, and you should display him to your utmost.

Cat shows offer the opportunity to create an imaginative display setting for your cat: the cage *must* be covered on top, floor and three sides, so why not create an attractive design? Some shows offer prizes for the best display. These can be fun to create, but the ones that win remind me of the costumes created for Arabian Horse Costume Classes: they are so elaborate and glittery that one scarcely sees the animal through all the paraphernalia.

Use colors that will flatter your cat, and try to keep in mind future colors you might show. For example, a deeper shade of a cat's eye color can really bring out the eyes. The worst possible display has a dark cat on dark flooring — the cat just disappears. A white cat on white material is also a mistake; either the cat or the cloth will look dirty.

You should try to make your cage decorations two-way, usable in both single-size and double-size cages. Double cages are usually available to exhibitors for a few additional dollars. Most people who get them do so because they don't want their cat to be cramped. The cat immediately flops down in one corner and doesn't move from the spot all day long. However, the double cage does make a better display and for that reason alone might be worth the extra fee.

Cages vary slightly in size from one part of the country to another, and even from state to state. Find out the standard cage size in your area and make your cage curtains slightly larger.

Your cat's number should be on the cage so that spectators can look it up in the catalog. But many spectators will not buy a catalog or won't want to be continually referring to it. Why not put up a card in the corner of the cage that gives the name, breed, sex, age and color of your cat for the benefit of spectators?

If you have business cards printed up, put them out on top of the cage. You might also put out breed information sheets or brochures. Lots of people will pick these up and may become interested in the breed.

Most of your cards and flyers will be thrown away, but some people will save them and call you months or even years later.

Cat show classes and awards

Cat shows classes and awards are complicated and differ from one association to the next; the information given here is therefore merely a general introduction.

Perhaps the most confusing thing about cat shows to the casual onlooker is the presence of several judges and rings. A cat show will have three to five judges and rings. Each judge has his own judging ring, and the show will be described according to the number of rings, a "four-ring show," or a "ten-ring show." (A ten ring show will be held over two days, five rings each day.)

Each ring is in effect a separate cat show. The judge in that ring judges each cat in the show separately from the other rings and without reference to the awards given in those rings. The separate judging continues right to the end of the show, so that each judge chooses his own finals winners, which might well be different cats, or in a different order, than those chosen by the other judges.

The final placings will be accumulated so that one cat will then emerge as the best in the show. If none of the judges concur on their first-placed cat, it is possible for a cat that has placed second or third in every ring, or missed a ring entirely, to become the best in the show.

Shows are gradually changing. One day shows are now as common as two-day shows, and the veterinary check that was once necessary at every show is now seldom used.

During a two-day show, your cat will be judged by half the judges on the first day and the rest of the judges on the second day. Other two day shows are actually two entirely separate shows held "back to back" in the same location; you may then enter for one day or for both. Because of the travel expenses involved, most people will enter their cats on both days. TICA, the newest and most innovative of the cat associations, has pioneered the three-day show. The show begins Friday evening from 5:00pm or 6:00pm to around midnight, and continues Saturday and Sunday. The three-day show will have as many as seventeen rings – five Friday, six each on Saturday and Sunday.

Shows are invariably held on weekends. Hours are normally around 9:00 am to 5:00 pm, with the show hall opening around 7:30 am so that exhibitors will have a chance to set up their cages and touch up their grooming.

The basic show class is the *novice,* for cats which have never won a first place ribbon. Its counterpart for those cats that have won a first is the *open* class. All classes are divided by breed, sex and by color or color groups; these will be listed in the show rules of the governing association. The entry clerk will determine the correct class for your cat given its sex, color, age, and whether it is a novice, open, champion, or grand champion. Of course, not every class will be filled, and more often than not there is only one cat in some classes. For example, if you have the only cream Persian female open in the show, you are a separate class all by yourself, and will receive the blue ribbon for this class.

The novice class winner next competes with the open class winner of its sex for the winners ribbon, the award that leads to accumulation of a Championship (four winner's ribbons [ACFA] to six winner's ribbons [CFA]). Alternatively, points are assigned to the class placings (as in TICA) and these are accumulated towards a championship. Champions and grand champions do not compete for the winner's ribbon. To continue with the previous example, if no other cream Persian female opens or novices are being shown, you will get the winner's ribbon and, at the end of the first day (ACFA) or the end of the show (CFA), your cat will be a champion. In a move to make its championship award more meaningful, TICA now requires one final in addition to the necessary points.

The title of grand champion can be achieved in a single show only by the most exceptional cats. In CFA, a cat must be a champion before it even begins to accumulate points towards the title of grand champion. Cats earn points towards the two hundred required by defeating other champions. In ACFA, six finals under six different judges plus a total of sixteen winner's ribbons are required. In TICA, 1000 points with six finals from four different judges, including three in the Top Five (SP) or Top Ten (AB) are required (points are based on class and finals placings, not on cats defeated). In ACFA and TICA, additional titles can be acquired beyond the grand championship. For example, in TICA, a supreme grand champion is a cat that has gone from a "single" grand championship to a double grand, triple grand, quadruple grand, and finally supreme grand with 6000 points plus finals along the way, plus one Best Cat as a quadruple grand.

The next step up the pyramid at the show is for all cats, males and females, from all classes of the same *color* to compete for the best of color award. Best of color does not mean that the judge thought your cat had the best color of the cats in the class; it means the judge thought your cat was the best cat of that color – still within the breed or division, of course. Second and third place BOC are usually awarded as well. Some breeds are grouped into divisions of color, such as solid colors, tabby colors, bicolors. If best of division is awarded in the breed, the next step will be for the best of color winners to compete for best of division. Finally, the judge will award his best of breed and placings. All this will take place without any cats of the breed being moved from the judging ring. If the breed is a large one, it may be shown in sections, with those cats still in competition for the higher awards left in their cages while the remainder of the class is returned.

The breed classes are only a preliminary to the finals. Once a judge has judged all his shorthair or longhair cats (specialty) or all his cats (allbreed), he will pick his top five or ten cats of the entire show (the number in the finals depends on the number of cats competing). The process will be repeated for each of the four show divisions: kittens, altered cats, championship cats (unaltered adult cats), and household pets (domestics and pet purebreds).

Those placing near the top of their breeds will need to listen for their number to be called for the finals. In some associations the numbers are not called, and the announcer will tell exhibitors to "check their numbers for a kitten final in ring two." It is certainly possible to final a cat even if it did not receive the best of breed award – in some cases, even the third and fourth best of breed winners may make the finals.

The three purebred sections (cat, kitten and alter) never compete with each other: a kitten will never be shown against an alter.

Each association has different regulations, and if you intend to show you should spend the few dollars to buy the Show Rules. You should already have the association's address from the person you bought your kitten from, or you can call her to ask for it (or to explain certain show regulations).

If you want to show in an association in which your kitten or cat is not registered, you can usually do so on the basis of your CFA registration. In this case, you will have to register your cat right after the show if you want to be eligible for any of its wins. For example, if your cat wins four winner's ribbons and its championship in an ACFA show, but is not registered in ACFA, you must do so at once to earn the title.

Of purebred animal competitions, cat shows are undoubtedly the most complicated. No novice should hesitate to ask fellow-exhibitors about show regulations; you may even find someone who knows less about it than you do!

Above all, you must learn to lose gracefully, for no one, ever, wins all the time. And you must not complain *too* much about the judges and other exhibitors. Remember when you go to a show that everyone else is there because they think they have a chance to win, too – not just to provide lesser cats for *your* cat to defeat! Make some friends, have some fun, be prepared to lose and still have fun, and let those lovely rosettes be a bonus – not the only reason you are there.

Chapter Seven: *Advertising and Sales*

Finding buyers for your kittens

Advertising your kittens includes word of mouth, making contacts at shows, and using the media. There's no end to promotional schemes you can use: you can distribute breed information at shows, you can send cute spring-kitten shots to local newspapers, you can put up notices at supermarkets, veterinary clinics, and community clubs, you can advertise in national cat magazines, breed magazines, or your local paper.

One word of caution: never put your address on any advertising materials for local distribution. If you do, you'll be getting drop-by customers and window-shoppers, and, who knows, the possible thief. Always insist on a screening call first.

The purpose of advertising is, of couse, to sell cats and kittens. There are people in the cat fancy who look upon advertising techniques as beneath them: they don't want their kittens relegated to the status of *products*. I know breeders who are reluctant to talk to spectators at a show, not because they are stand-offish, but because they are afraid of being accused of hard-sell tactics. When lured into a conversation they will never, never mention any kittens for sale even if their cattery is bursting at the seams. There are others who, as long as they are able to place all their kittens, just don't want to make the effort. But remember: the more customers you can attract, the more choosy you can be about finding top-notch homes for your kittens.

Pet, breeder, or show buyer?

Determine at the outset whether your buyer wants a pet, a breeder, or a show-quality kitten. Your subsequent attitude will be different for each.

For the pet owner, play up your kittens for all they're worth. There is absolutely no point in going into the weaknesses of your line or of any particular kitten. Pet buyers will invariably misunderstand. If you say that you just can't get proper ear-set on your cats, they'll think this means that your cats have deformed ears. They won't realize that you're talking about an ideal; in fact, many would be surprised that a written standard exists. "This kitten has a weak chin, that one's tail is too short." In your zeal to be fair and honest, you can go too far. The pet owner who pays $150 or $225 – a small fortune relative to the kitten-market in general – doesn't want to know that he's getting less than ideal chins and tails. He will value his kitten less *to no purpose.* On the other hand, you don't want to give the impression that his kitten could be a top show winner either. You might point out that show cats are a very small percentage of all purebred cats and that they sell for $500 and up.

Playing up the good points rather than the bad ones does not apply to any deformity, which should be pointed out and its implications explained to the potential buyer.

The best way to give your customer an idea of what he's buying is to show him the mother and father, or pictures of them, and explain that the kitten will probably turn out like them. All kittens are cute and cuddly, but cats spend ninety percent of their lives as adults, so be sure the potential buyer likes the parents.

Breeding kittens are those you *could* allow to go for pets, unless they are essential to your breeding plan. Breeding kittens can be advertised in breed newsletters, including a pedigree and photo. Buyers will be interested in it primarily for its pedigree. You might also find people interested in breeding through local newspaper advertising; these will be newcomers to the breed and you can have a lot of fun helping them get started; they can be particularly useful to your breeding program if they choose to work exclusively with your lines. For example, you can get a kitten back from one of the females you sell by providing stud service. The buyer thus becomes an extension of your own breeding program.

Selling a kitten to an experienced breeder, should you reach those heights, is your easiest sale. The breeder knows all the right questions to ask and should have no unreasonable expectations. But selling a kitten to the beginner who's interested in breeding or showing will require all the time you can spare to advise them concerning your bloodlines, their kitten's good points and bad, possible mates, the problems and expenses of breeding, and so forth. You must be even more careful selling to a beginner who wants to show. The person who breeds can hope for better kittens, but the show-oriented buyer can feel stuck with a cat that doesn't win.

If you have a kitten of really superior quality that you can't keep for yourself, you must make every effort to sell it to someone who will show it, thus promoting your cattery. You may want to retain breeding access to it as well. Selling to a show home can be difficult if you're not well known. You may occasionally find a local customer interested in showing. But your best bet is to keep the kitten until it's old enough to show (four months) and enter it in a show or two yourself. In this way, you will know if it is *truly* show quality. It's all too easy to decide that the best kitten in a litter is show quality, just because it looks so nice compared to the others. Give it a real trial before you sell it to someone as show potential; if anyone must be embarrassed by your faulty judgment, let it be yourself. If the kitten does well at one or two shows, *then* advertise it in a breed magazine or newsletter. Send the prospective buyer its show record, pedigree, price, and a good photograph. You may even find a buyer at the show. Most show catalogs will list which kittens or cats are for sale along with the price.

Conditions of purchase

Some breeders try to attach conditions to every kitten sale they make. Of course, it is important to ensure that pet kittens will be properly altered, and the buyer of a pet kitten should have no objection, although even here provision might be made for the buyer who later decides that he wants to raise one or two litters.

For a kitten sold to a novice as a breeder, you as the seller might want to ask for pick-of-litter of the cat's first litter after mating to one of your own studs; you would provide the stud service free of charge. Once again, the buyer should have no real objections, since he is getting a free stud service and will also have the benefit of your experience for what might be his first litter of kittens. In the case of a male kitten to be used at stud, you might ask for a reduced-fee breeding from him.

Conditions such as these are a way of insuring that you have access to your own bloodlines at a future date, should your own cats die or prove incapable of breeding. Other sorts of conditions, however, are nothing but a burden to the buyer and should not be imposed.

Show quality kittens, in particular, are sometimes sold with so many strings attached that the purchaser feels she is obligating herself for the rest of her life – or at least the cat's life. An example: no kittens produced by this cat or by this cat's kittens shall ever be sold within the region. Another example: the seller wants unlimited stud service free of charge to the male kitten he has sold.

If a buyer pays a fair price for a kitten, he should be able to use that kitten however he wants. Conditions attached to the sale should never extend beyond a year or two, and these should be carefully spelled out in advance so that no misunderstandings and hurt feelings ensue. Requests are one thing, demands are another. If you've been careful about who you sold a kitten to, both are unnecessary.

Trades and payment plans

Beware of the trade. "I'll send you a kitten of *x* color or from *x* bloodlines and you send me one of *x*." Trader A sends a kitten and waits two or three years – or forever – for the kitten from Trader B. And it's not even B's fault: his queens haven't produced the hoped-for kitten so he has nothing to send. Or Trader A feels taken because the kitten he sent was much nicer quality than the one he received from B. Except between very good friends – and usually even then – a cash price on each kitten is the best idea; from a legal standpoint, the only idea.

What about selling kittens on the payment plan? I know a few people who do this regularly. Buyers do not expect it, though, and collecting and keeping track of payments is annoying. Except between friends, I would not recommend it.

Once your cats become successful, you may even find that people are sending you money in the mail as down payments on kittens not yet born. They are hoping that you will accept the money and then be obligated to sell them a kitten. If this happens to you, consider carefully before you accept the money. It's much, much easier to send it back now than later!

The classified ad

Since, as a novice breeder, most if not all your kittens will be sold as pets, I'm going to cover pet kitten sales in some detail.

Usually your best bet will be an ad in the local newspaper or the nearest large-city newspaper. Your category will be Pets, Purebred Pets, or Purebred Cats if your paper breaks them down. There are always very few purebred cats compared to dogs being advertised. You will want to include your kitten's breed, the price, and your phone number as the absolute minimum. Not including the price will bring innumerable calls from people looking for $5 kittens. Also consider the following:

(1) Registered. Not all purebreds are registered, and many buyers will see registration as a guarantee of pure bloodlines, plus a bit of added prestige. You could also put "CFA registered" or "double registered," but this is likely to be confusing, since many people aren't aware that there is more than one registering body for cats.

(2) Champion-sired, champion bloodlines, and so forth. Of course almost any purebred kitten has some champions in its pedigree, but the kitten buyer sometimes thinks that a champion means the best, perhaps the best in the country.

(3) All shots. This will be attractive to the buyer since it means he will save some time and money.

(4) Guaranteed healthy. Only, of course, if you *do* have a clearly-defined health guarantee. If you use this in your ad, you must be careful to spell out the terms of the guarantee to anyone who buys a kitten, even if he doesn't ask; otherwise, you could find people trying to return a cat two years later!

(5) Adorable, fluffy, cute. These are good persuaders for giving away free kittens, but the space can be better used when you're selling purebreds.

(6) Box-trained or litter-trained. Here again, largely unnecessary. The buyer of a purebred has almost always had cats before and knows that there is very little "training" involved.

The phone call

A potential customer has seen your ad and gives you a call. The call is a vital connection between your advertising program, no matter how meager, and your kitten sales. Some people will be so eager to buy a kitten that they won't be turned away by anything you may say over the phone. Others will just be curious about what a Maine Coon cat might be ("is it really part racoon?").

My experience has been that about half the phone calls I get will result in a sale. Almost all the people who arrange to come out will do so, and almost everyone who gets in the door will buy a kitten. Once that furry-purry bundle is in their arms, the kitten virtually sells itself. Therefore, your primary sales objective is the phone call.

Normally you will want to identify yourself as a breeder, and explain briefly what sexes, ages and colors you have to choose from. If you intend to do any screening (and you should), now is the time – not when they're in your home. An easy and excellent way to screen buyers is to ask if they've had a cat before. Find out how long it lived and what it died from. If it was run over by a car, find another buyer. If it died recently of a contagious disease, find out (from your vet) if the disease organisms could still be present in their household. If they have a cat or dog already, find out if they're prepared for the problems of introducing a new pet. Do they have small children that could injure a kitten? Do they intend to have their kitten altered, and if not, why not? If they insist on a male or female, why? Ask about anything else you feel is important. The answers to these questions will reveal much about the potential buyer's attitude towards cats. If you feel the person is unsuitable, tell him you don't think any of your kittens would be suitable for him.

You may get calls from people who just like to chat about cats, or tell you all about their pet cat, so try to sort the wheat from the chaff and avoid a long conversation. People who are truly interested in buying will want to come out and look, not just talk over the phone. Also, other customers may be trying to call on the line that's tied up.

When giving directions to your house, insist on a definite time; otherwise you could find yourself hanging around home waiting for someone who will never show up.

Before visitors arrive you'll want to make a quick check on litter box cleanliness and the current state of the kittens' bottoms. Be sure you have all the papers relating to kitten sales at hand. These might include: a litter-record notebook, a receipt book, information sheet on kitten care, alteration agreement, pedigree. I usually give some food samples, too, and keep cardboard carriers handy in case the purchaser doesn't bring one.

You could keep a presentation book prepared with your best cat and kitten photographs, pedigrees of current breeding stock, championship certificates, and so forth.

The health guarantee

First, you should know that when you sell a kitten, its good health is *implied by law* and you could be forced to refund the purchase price if the buyer can prove that the kitten was unhealthy at the time of sale. This is true whether of not you give any health guarantee.

If the health of your cats is a priority, as it should be, you can emphasize this to your buyers. Good health is one area where the purebred-kitten buyer can save a bundle by buying from a breeder. But be sure you turn over a parasite-free, completely immunized kitten to the new owner! If the kitten *has* had any health problems, explain them carefully and perhaps make a deduction from the price, and if the kitten needs its final shots, write this down for the purchaser. I offer to give the final shots myself. This allows me to see the kitten again a couple of weeks after the sale and talk to the owner about any problems he may be having.

An acceptable health guarantee from both the buyer's and seller's points of view: the kitten can be returned within three days of purchase if it has been examined by a vet and its health is not satisfactory. In addition, I would offer a refund or replacement for a kitten that died or became permanently ill if the source of the problem was probably my cattery, whatever the length of time; for example, in the case of a death from congenital heart defects.

The visit

When customers arrive, you'll want to show them photographs and pedigrees of the parents before bringing out the kittens. You could also bring out the mother if she is looking well (some tend to look rather scraggly after nursing a big litter). Mothers will tend to ignore their babies if they are shown together, and people will sometimes conclude that she's been a bad mother or even that you are trying to pass off some other cat's kittens as hers!

You should leave one or two adults out in the room, especially those in top condition or those with attractive personalities. This way the purchaser has a chance to see an adult of the same bloodlines without being confronted by a huge herd of cats. A mob of cats will lower the value of each one in the eyes of a kitten purchaser.

When you bring out the kittens check that they are completely clean and take out no more than three at a time. During your introductory conversation you will probably have gotten some idea of what the customer wants and will know best which kittens to show him. Present each kitten separately and give its sex and color. To you, each kitten is a separate identity. To the buyer, they tend to look alike. As soon as he has chosen a kitten, put the others away or he may change his mind after all the papers are made out.

The sale

Once a customer has chosen a kitten, hand him a cattery card so he can make out a check while you write his receipt. Most buyers will want to pay by check; few of these will be bad, but it does no harm to ask for identification. If you require cash, you should have said so during the phone conversation. Write the buyer's name and address into the records you keep of each litter. Then go over any special conditions of sale, the health guarantee, transfer of papers, and so forth.

You will also want to review the first few days of adjustment. In particular, I advise that the kitten be kept confined to one room until he is definite on the location of his litter box, and I also suggest feeding what he is used to for at least a few days. A photocopied flyer with suggestions on feeding, bathing, grooming and so forth is an excellent idea. You can include space for the kitten's birth-date, color, etc., if you are not giving registration papers with it.

The complaints or lack of complaints you get later on are a good indication of how you're doing. Try to follow up all sales with a phone call a week or so later, and another after a month or two. Many people will not call you even though they have minor problems they need help with; a few will pester you contin-ually. I like to emphasize to buyers that I'm concerned for the ongoing welfare of all my cats and kittens. I usually ask that they contact me first if they should ever have to sell or give away their cat. I *don't* guarantee that I'll take it back myself, but I *can* help in finding a new home. I'd much rather see a cat eutha-nized than placed in a bad home or deserted.

Other points to emphasize

If your kittens are people-oriented, outgoing little critters, say so. I've bought twelve-week-old kittens from breeders that had no idea how to interact with humans. Pick them up and they'd fight, squirm and scratch to get away. Put them down and they'd run under the nearest cover, trembling. Such kittens can be gentled, but only at the expense of endless time, patience and understanding — more than most pet buyers would be willing to give, or will know how to give. If you have a kitten that is shy and timid, be sure to say so. Some people will treasure such a cat all the more; others will feel cheated when they discover their kitten's personality.

People will value their pets more if you can cite a few illustrious ancestors; there is no reason why you shouldn't brag about the pedigree. Whether or not to hand out pedigrees with your pet kittens is up to you. The pedigree is meaning-less to the pet buyer except for its prestige value. I once had a kitten buyer return a kitten because he'd looked at the pedigree when he got home and noticed that the mother and father were half-siblings (had the same sire). He could not be persuaded that an "inbred" kitten could be perfectly normal and healthy.

On the subject of prices, be perfectly clear from the very first phone call. If you've advertised kittens at $150 up and have only one left at $250, say so immediately.

Refunds

Whatever your stated policy, you'll do best not to argue with the buyer who wants to return a kitten within a week or two of sale *whatever* the reason. If you sold the kitten at a fair price, you should be able to resell it at that price. Depending on why a refund is requested, you might be justified in deducting from it the cost of advertising the kitten again.

The purchaser of a kitten to be used for breeding expects more than the pet buyer. Sometimes she runs into problems when the cat matures and for one reason or another does not reproduce. In such instances the buyer might think she's entitled to a refund or replacement. Sometimes veterinary advice has been sought and the vet may have told the purchaser not to breed because cat the is too small, too fat, too thin, or too much this-or-that.

The breeder's only obligation in such cases, provided she has sold a kitten in good health and with no known problems that would complicate breeding, is to provide the purchaser with expert advice. A breeding-quality kitten is just that, bred or not, and some kitten buyers are willing to pay the extra money for the better quality even though they do *not* intend to breed cats.

In short, it is ridiculous for the breeder to have to guarantee not only the kitten's health and quality at time of sale, but the cat's continuing health and development, its lack of personality problems, its fertility, reproductive capacity, instinct for motherhood and milk supply long after the kitten has left her cattery. The buyer of a kitten that grows up to be a problem cat may well find the breeder to be willing to help out in other ways, but she should not *demand* compensation she's not entitled to. If breeders had to guarantee every aspect of their cats throughout their lifetimes, few would ever sell a kitten. Once again, congenital defects are the exception.

A mature cat sold as a proven queen or stud is another matter entirely, and the buyer and seller should clearly work out exactly what is guaranteed. A written agreement, even if it's just a hand-written note, is always a good idea.

The importance of pet kittens

Pet kittens are the basis of the cat breeding hobby; they are also the most rewarding sales you can make. No matter how interested you become in showing, you must always keep in mind the market for which you are producing and the product that market demands. If you do, you will never be tempted to breed a kitten that cannot function normally. *You* may be willing to put up with the problems associated with very-extreme breeding, but will the average pet owner? Far better the producer of mediocre, non-registered but vigorous kittens than the "best-in-show" breeder who makes life miserable for the cats she breeds and the people she sells them to.

Appendix

ACA (American Cat Association)
10065 Foothill Rd, Lake View Terrace CA 91342

ACC (American Cat Council)
PO Box 662 Pasadena, CA 91102

ACFA (American Cat Fanciers Association)
PO Box 203, Point Lookout MO 65726

CCA (Canadian Cat Association)
14 Nelson St West, Suite 5, Brampton, Ontario, Canada L6X 1B7

CFA (Cat Fanciers Association)
1309 Allaire Av, Ocean NJ 07712

CFF (Cat Fanciers Federation)
9509 Montgomery Rd, Cinncinnati, Ohio 45242

CCFF (Crown Cat Fanciers Federation)
PO Box 34, Nazareth, KY 40048

TICA (The International Cat Association)
P.O. Box 2988, Harlingen, Texas 78551

UCF (United Cat Federation)
6621 Thornwood St, San Diego CA 92111

The Book of the Cat edited by Michael Wright & Sally Walters. Summit Books: New York, 1980. The best of many cat cyclopedias.

The Cat by Muriel Beade. Simon & Schuster: New York, 1977. Emphasis on cat behaviour and biology; draws on recent research.

The Well Cat Book by Terri McGinnis, DVM. Random House: New York, 1975. Cat's anatomy, home examination, and index of signs are useful.

Feline Medicine and Surgery Second Edition, edited by E J Catcott, DVM, PhD. American Veterinary Publications, 1975. Standard veterinary textbook on cats.

The CFA Yearbook. Published annually by the Cat Fanciers Association. Huge volume packed with full-color photos (advertisements) for show cats and catteries; also special history and breed articles.

The Silent Miaow by Paul Gallico. Crown Printing: New York, 1964. Information for felines on how to conquer human hearts and homes. Readers will also enjoy Gallico's novel, *The Abandoned.*

Alteration Agreement

As part of the purchase agreement for the kitten or cat born _____,
breed, color and sex described as follows_____,
the buyer promises to have it altered as soon as it is old enough, and no later than
_____(date).

If seller does not receive verification of altering within thirty days after the date indicated above, an additional payment of $_____ shall be immediately due and payable.

The buyer promises to provide responsible care for the kitten or cat, including protection from hazards such as traffic, dogs, and small children. The buyer agrees to notify the seller if the kitten or cat is resold or given away.

Seller reserves the right to repossess the kitten in the event of failure or refusal of buyer to comply with the terms of this agreement.

Seller agrees to deliver the kitten's registration papers to buyer within _____ days of (1) valid notification of altering, or (2) receipt of the stated additional payment.   Date _____

Signed _____
                                          Buyer

Address _____

_____

Phone _____

_____
                                          Seller

Address _____

_____

Phone _____

Stud Service Agreement

Name of Stud_____CFA #_____

       Breed_____Color_____Eye Color_____

Name of Queen_____CFA #_____

       Breed_____Color_____Eye Color_____

_____, the queen's owner, agrees to pay to _____, the stud's owner, the sum of $_____ and/or _____ pick of litter in return for stud service from the stud named above to the queen named above.

During the time the queen is boarded, the stud's owner will take reasonable care of the queen but will not be liable for any injury to the queen.

The owner of the queen will pay for board at the rate of _____ per day beginning with the _____ day the queen is boarded.

The queen's owner will be responsible for any veterinary bills incurred on the queen's behalf while boarded with the stud's owner.

If the queen does not conceive during her initial visit, the queen's owner has the right to return her twice under this agreement. If she still does not conceive after three visits, _____% ($_____) of the total stud fee will be forfeited to the stud's owner and the remainder ($_____) refunded to the queen's owner.

The stud's owner has the right to visit or send a representative to the queen's cattery to see the kittens resulting from the above mating. The stud's owner or representative will designate _____ pick kitten at the age of eight weeks and agrees to take that kitten as fulfillment of the stud fee.

In the event the queen has only one surviving kitten, the total stud fee will be reduced to $_____, or the queen can be returned for a free stud service, at the stud's owner's choice.

_____% ($_____) of the total stud fee will be due when the queen is returned to her owner after a successful mating, and the remaining _____% ($_____) when the resulting kittens are _____ weeks old.

Dated this _____ day of _____, 19_____.

_____   _____
       Owner of Stud   *Owner of Queen*

Witnessed by _____

Litter Record

Litter #_____CFA Litter Registration #_____

Queen _____

Stud _____

Stud's Owner_____

Date of Breeding_____ Date Delivered_____ Gestation_____days

Notes on Pregnancy and Delivery:_____

_____

_____

Vaccinations of Kittens:

Date_____ Type_____ Serial #_____

Date_____ Type_____ Serial #_____

Date_____ Type_____ Serial #_____

	Sex	Color	Sold To	Date	Price	Alteration Agreement
1						
2						
3						
4						
5						
6						

Stud Booking

Stud _____ CFA Reg # _____

Date of Contact _____

Name of Queen _____

Date of Birth _____ CFA Reg # _____ Ch Status _____

Sire _____

Dam _____

Owner _____

     Address _____

     _____

     Phone _____

Name of Vet _____

     Address _____

     _____

     Phone _____

Date of Vaccination _____

FeLeuk: Pos Neg

Date Sent:

(1) _____ Bred _____

(2) _____ Bred _____

(3) _____ Bred _____

Type of Contract _____

Payment Received _____

_____

Kitten Received _____

Number of Kittens Born _____ Males _____ Females _____

Kittens' Quality _____

Additional Notes _____

_____

_____

Index